T0039780

BEPPE GAMBETTA
THE FLATPICKING SOURCEBOOK

Translated by Alex Giarbini.
Proofread by Mike Kaufman.
Edited by David Harrison.
Cover photograph by Michael Schlueter.

Order No. AM1011098
Printed in the EU.

To acces audio visit:
www.halleonard.com/mylibrary
Enter Code:

6897-6251-3528-5415

ISBN: 978-1-78558-078-9

For all works contained herein:
Unauthorized copying, arranging, adapting, recording, internet posting, public performance,
or other distribution of the music in this publication is an infringement of copyright.
Infringers are liable under the law.

Visit Hal Leonard Online at
www.halleonard.com

Contact us:
Hal Leonard
7777 West Bluemound Road
Milwaukee, WI 53213
Email: info@halleonard.com

In Europe, contact:
Hal Leonard Europe Limited
42 Wigmore Street
Marylebone, London, W1U 2RY
Email: info@halleonardeurope.com

In Australia, contact:
Hal Leonard Australia Pty. Ltd.
4 Lentara Court
Cheltenham, Victoria, 3192 Australia
Email: info@halleonard.com.au

I would like to express my warmest thanks to my wife Federica Calvino Prina, a classical guitarist and dance historian, for her love and skill transforming my notes of a life on the road into a true book.

PREFACE

*Anyone who is committed to traditional music or roots music
is destined by nature to become a teacher or an educator.*

*Traditional music has been passed down orally for generations,
in a direct and spontaneous way. Likewise, on my musical journey,
though in more modern times, I have developed a sensibility and
learned many things from magical moments during my travels.*

*I have decided to write, and make available to acoustic guitar
students, my teaching experience as a musician on the road, in order to
fill a gap in published methods. I have taken old concepts, updating
previous methods to present needs, with the intention of inspiring
new and old generations to undertake a musical journey that, I believe,
can still generate lots of good music and beautiful moments to share.*

*This book is inspired by my artistic path, based on the emotions
I have felt during these years of music on the road and the numerous
experiences of teaching, researching, and producing independent music.*

*As many already said, teaching implies being a bearer of knowledge,
but it also involves never losing sight of passion and wonder for content
which represents art and must be treated accordingly.*

*There is no special recipe for writing a book that teaches both
technique and love for good music. This is an attempt to combine
these two elements, a synthesis of many experiences and
previous works that are, after all, a diary of my life as an artist.*

*The underlying theme of the course has been strictly
and passionately to analyze different repertoires, first in their
own context and then—giving space to imagination and creativity—
going beyond simple reproduction. There is indeed a common
thread of poetry as well as technique that combines
repertoires inspired by folk and urban traditions.*

*Following this thread and weaving it in different ways you may
discover unexplored parts of your own creativity on a journey that
takes you far away from the artistic templates served up by
the so-called mainstream of the mass media.*

*Through this autobiographical approach developed over the years,
I hope to encourage fresh enthusiasm for the acoustic guitar, and
to satisfy the students in the courses, seminars and workshops
I have taught and still teach in the US, in Italy and around the world.
I dedicate this work to them with my deepest affection.*

Beppe Gambetta

Photo by *Jerry Herring*

BIOGRAPHY

*Beppe Gambetta has transformed journeying into an art form.
Now acknowledged at an international level, he is considered by
the American masters as the European leader in flatpicking acoustic guitar.
He has gained full recognition by his American counterparts, as a
prominent keeper of an eternally evolving musical tradition.*

*With America in his heart, and his roots deeply anchored in the sun
and the olive trees of the Mediterranean area, Gambetta connects the shores
of the two continents with great ease. Thanks to his early travels and studies
in the '80s, Beppe chose a path that brought him to explore not only
Europe and North America, but also Australia and South America.*

*He has researched and revived the music of 20th Century Italian virtuosi.
He brings a unique touch of poetry with which he composes and
arranges acoustic music, adding his own taste and sensibility.*

*He has performed in concert all over the world—from the
Ryman Auditorium in Nashville to the Metropolitan Museum of Art
in New York—from the days of the 'Iron Curtain' as part of
Czechoslovakian Festivals, to contemporary Canadian and
Australian Festivals, Argentinian shows dedicated to emigrants
and the Genovese Acoustic Nights which have been attracting
thousands of spectators over the last fourteen years.*

*Beppe Gambetta had the honour of meeting Pete Seeger
and of playing with Doc Watson; he met Fabrizio De Andrè
(famed Italian artist) and has recorded with artists such
David Grisman, Norman Blake, Dan Crary, Gene Parsons,
Mike Marshall and Darrell Scott...*

*As his main mission, he has devoted part of his career to teaching
his art at several international schools and, twenty-two years ago,
he founded one of the first European acoustic guitar camps.*

www.beppegambetta.com

Contents

Introduction

This book deals with an acoustic guitar style which, in the American tradition, is known as *flatpicking*. The same style can also be found in various other forms, but without any specific definition, in many European traditions, and even worldwide.

The American term flatpicking originates from "picking on a flat-top guitar" (as opposed to an arch-top guitar, generally used by jazz musicians). The flat-top acoustic guitar has been played by great artists who have left us a wide and varied repertoire. It is an instrument capable of transmitting rhythm, poetry and passion; it can keep unforgettable popular themes alive; and it can accompany songwriters and provide them with ideas for composing and arranging inspired melodies.

The style of flatpicking can be studied by following infinite variations reaching as far as the traditional schools of the most remote corners of the world, going back in time to bygone ages and the masters of the past.

Using traditional forms as a basis, this book in part also traces the evolution and stylistic changes of repertoire, deriving from forces such as urbanization, folk revival, cultural importation and contamination, fashions and trends—phenomena that often underlie major changes.

These techniques and the aesthetics they are played with are not just a heritage for a strict circle of adherents but they are actually important points of reference: they are the "great mothers", a starting point for developing new synergies, and also constitute a reference point for those who thoroughly intend to explore guitar in other, diverse directions.

In this work, the school of reference is American flatpicking because this specific style is linked to some prominent musical genres, from early Country Music to Bluegrass and lots of other branches of overseas popular music. Among the flatpicking styles of these "roots" it is the one that has generated the largest number of significant artists who have influenced musicians—even those of faraway cultures—worldwide.

The purpose of this book, however, is to offer a journey into the world of acoustic flatpicking guitar, analyzing and comparing examples from different traditions with an open, imartial approach.

Following various encounters over the years comparing teaching experiences of different artists, it has become clear that studying acoustic guitar is a very free and creative path that does not follow strict technical rules. The artist is free to interpret these techniques and develop them according to his own instinct and physical characteristics. The good teacher is the one who favours access to a free form of expression.

This is the most common teaching approach, so beyond the obvious and essential rules, many teachers advise their students to freely choose the technical details that generate the most satisfying sound. The famous phrase "whatever makes your guitar play in the best way, is the right technique" is a recurring comment I totally agree with.

If this freedom of choice is handled with a careful critical and artistic approach, it can generate exellence and it will characterize the musician's personality. This is the direction I suggest you should follow with the help of this book.

A Lesson from the Past

Many of the styles linked to traditional music have a common element: the guitar has evolved in different stages from an accompanying instrument to a solo instrument.

This has occurred thanks to the personality and genius of the great guitarists who have shaped styles and techniques in order to express the earliest forms of solo. Today these artists are respected as the fathers, the mentors of this style, being able to influence and inspire new generations with their art.

The musician who had this leading role in the American tradition was Doc Watson, a legendary guitarist from Deep Gap, North Carolina. Thanks to an extremely long career, he was able to connect younger generations with the rich and essential aesthetics of the Old Time music; nowadays the study of his music is a must for everyone interested in the genre. The other recognized fathers of flatpicking guitar are Norman Blake, Tony Rice, Clarence White and Dan Crary. In my opinion nothing can be more fulfilling than listening to and studying the music of the fathers.

I wish I could describe the most exciting moments of my life on the road when I had the chance to meet some of those "fathers" and, despite the limits of words, could convey the joy and the artistic and spiritual enrichment I have experienced.

I met Doc Watson on many occasions. Blind from birth, he was able to capture sounds and moods with a highly-developed sixth sense. This allowed him to feel his audience and offer positive feedback to those around him. Playing with him in the quiet of a backstage room, I had first-hand proof of his artistic stature. His harmonies were apparently simple; but no one else will ever be able to capture them with the same essential beauty. Doc Watson spoke with the voice of an wise old man and he knew how to encourage you. When you shook hands with him, you were surprised by his rough hands and you learned that, despite his handicap and his age, he always worked in the fields surrounding his house. Likewise, Pete Seeger, the father of folk revival, who proudly showed the European-style dry-stone walls he personally built around his house, had calloused hands. At the age of ninety, brimming with energy, he would get out of the little electric car which he drove into town for shopping. His words would relentlessly flow with memories, stories and ideas of all kinds among which there was wide room for projects and plans for the future. One of these ideas stands out: that of making the world a better place, fairer for everyone using art and music as a means to move people. He would grab his guitar and talk about the etymology of nouns, explaining that in India "tar" means string.

Rough fingers hardened by labour start a bass line and Pete played a couple of simple chords in dropped D tuning while explaining his technique when accompanying a song. After so many years, in a quiet corner of his home, his class and his groove were still extremely moving. Notes resounded with the same intensity as when, every night, thousands of spellbound people would sing along with him in songs and hymns of hope.

I have to stop here because this was not meant to be my memoirs. Still, these are unforgettable moments offered to me by art and experienced not only in America (the memory of my brief encounters with Fabrizio De Andrè still fascinate me). Such profound experiences have persuaded me to keep this ideal rapport with the music of the fathers alive and to suggest this path as an important passage in the artistic experience of each musician.

I think it is educationally enlightening to acknowledge the fathers, and, at the same time, to follow the evolutionary pattern created by new generations of teachers who have developed a style with innovative ideas.

Simplifying to an extreme degree, the path of swing stretches from Eddie Lang to Django Reinhardt and Birelli Lagrene; while the path of fingerpicking guitar goes from John Fahey to Leo Kottke and Michael Hedges; flatpicking guitar goes from Delmore Brothers to Doc Watson, Tony Rice and Brian Sutton; Celtic music goes from Dick Gaughan, to Artie McGlinn, Tony McManus, and so on.

In conclusion, besides listening, it is also essential to learn and take in every detail of some of the historical masterpieces. Nowadays it is much easier than in former times to come across printed material with music notation. Still, in my opinion, some music needs to be transcribed directly by the student, because the process of personally transcribing the music of other musicians leads to a more conscious assimilation.

For this purpose, I have included a crucial bibliography and discography. I have preferred to cite them in each chapter in order to diversify the sources and best enhance each topic.

Recommended Biography:
Kent Gustavson,
Blind But Now I see (biography of Doc Watson),
Blooming Twig Books 2010

Recommended Recordings:
Doc Watson, *On Stage*, Vanguard 1982
Norman Blake, *Whiskey Before Breakfast*, Rounder
Tony Rice, *Cold on the Shoulder*, Rounder 1983
Clarence White, *Clarence White and the Kentucky Colonels*, Rounder
Dan Crary, *Jammed If I Do*, Sugar Hill 1994

Fundamentals

Right Hand—Searching for Tone

When developing and combining the different elements that produce the sound and give it colour, the great masters show a refinement that distinguishes them from all the others. The right hand controls the tone, the rhythm and the dynamics. These elements are developed through endless experimentation and alterations—often minute— in terms of, touch, fingering, angles, pressure, type of movement, relaxation, materials and gauges used for strings and picks. The critical factors here are the grip and the pick direction. This also include the way the right hand rests, the angle and the point at which the string is touched. The shape and the material of the pick also contribute to the sound. The gauge of the pick should vary from medium to heavy and extra heavy, the shapes ranging from drop to triangular, while the materials can range from nylon to new and sophisticated plastic compositions which have in recent years, reached the quality of turtle shell picks. The majority of guitarists play with the tip of the pick, but a minority prefer the fuller and warmer tone of the rounded part.

Pick Gripping and Hand Rest

The most common way to hold a pick is with two fingers, between the thumb and the side of the index finger (without holding the pick with the softer, fleshy part of the fingertip). For different reasons (better control, better balance, instinct...) a minority of guitarists (including me) tend to hold the pick with three fingers. The fingers that are not holding the pick should be held in a relaxed position towards the inside of the palm of the hand. Guitarists generally state that the best way to hold the pick is how they have chosen to do it. This implies that holding the pick is a very personal choice.

Resting the right hand on the soundboard during solos (but not while playing a rhythm please!) is a technique common to almost all acoustic guitarists using a traditional approach, adopted in order to increase precision, sound control and power. The most common hand rest is that of the little finger (or little finger and ring finger together) on the pickguard.

Another type of hand rest involves placing the palm on the bridge, anchored in the low strings, but very lightly in order to avoid choking the sound. To facilitate both this type of rest and the percussive movement that I use in some of my songs, I invented the Beppe Gambetta wrist rest which many acoustic guitarists have already adopted. The alternation and combination of the two types of rest described above is very useful.

Basic Movements

Technically, the right hand can pick strings using three types of movement: wrist, arm and fingers.
• The movement of the wrist (more-or-less rotary) is usually the most substantial element in picking and is used by the majority of guitarists.
• The movement of the arm is used when playing the rhythm, but rarely when soloing because it is too wide and difficult to control (but there are exceptions— Doc Watson, for example, was able to use his arm in solos as well).
• The careful and delicate movement of the fingers is the finishing touch, the means to handle tone refinements and techniques such as string skipping, appoggiaturas and crosspicking.

It is interesting to notice that there is a connection between aesthetics of the movement and beauty of the sound, as an aesthetically elegant and fluid motion almost always produces an equally good sound.

Those who want to deepen their research into perfect touch may draw inspiration from classical guitar technique, applying it where appropriate in their own playing. According to academic studies the four phases identified in sound production are: *attack*, *decay*, *sustain* and *release* before the next note. A careful analysis of these four phases can produce great progress. Specifically in flatpicking guitar, the *attack* (the length of time the pick spends on the string before plucking) is of foremost importance as it may create a rhythmic heaviness if prolonged.

Left Hand

The left hand fingers of acoustic guitarists never create the perpendicular angle to the neck typical of classical guitarists, because they need a minimum angle in order togive rhythm, power and natural feel to notes played with pull-offs, hammer-ons and other techniques.

At the same time, for a modern and comprehensive musical approach, they have to be able to cover at least five frets in each fingering position. For this reason stretching exercises and an accurate and well-considered position are required.

The thumb should be placed at the same height as the middle finger, slightly visible behind the fretboard (it may also be used to fret strings on the fretboard). The wrist helps to keep the hand in position at a relaxed angle. Fretting notes with the very tip of your fingers is, like in any other guitar trick, essential for a good left hand technique.

Warm-Up and Workout

The warm-up is the initial phase of practice—the preparation for the actual musical exercise. It is also used to warm your fingers up before a gig: to prepare your hand for the extraordinary physical effort that flatpicking guitar requires.

The process is simple: all bad hand positions and choked sounds have to be corrected. This approach helps to develop a fundamental skill of the self-taught guitarist: the ability to self-criticise. Each movement can be enriched and widely varied by playing from slow to fast, from hard to soft, syncopated, staccato, muted, played with down-strokes only, or with up-strokes (when possible), etc.

And, of course, your friend the metronome will help maintain your accuracy. Generally, each exercise has a specific technical purpose and the breadth of acoustic guitar workout exercises deserves a separate publication.

I have developed a selection of six exercises that focus on the technical aspects that I consider as fundamental. However, the topics that have not been covered may be further explored using different sources.

The right hand in particular should be given special attention in practicing any type of string skipping or combination (it will become very useful as you progress to go through the chapters on strumming on p. 27 and Crosspicking on p. 51).

For the left hand I would recommend to add changes of position, stretching out on five or six frets, silent movements, resistance marathons, playing entire songs with the left hand only and doing exercises with fingers anchored to the fretboard.

Recommended Bibliography:
Jody Fisher, *Guitar Workout*, Alfred Publishing
Glenn Kurtz, *Practicing*, Vintage Books 2007

Single String Workout

This approach will teach you to control the simplest movement on a single string.

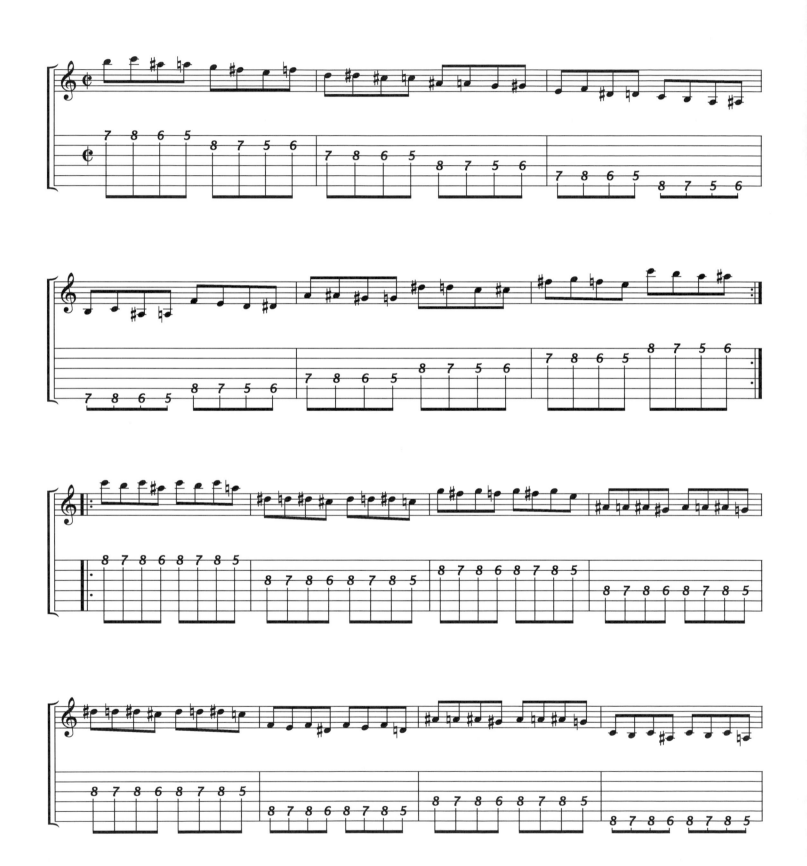

© 2010 Beppe Gambetta (SIAE - ITALIA)

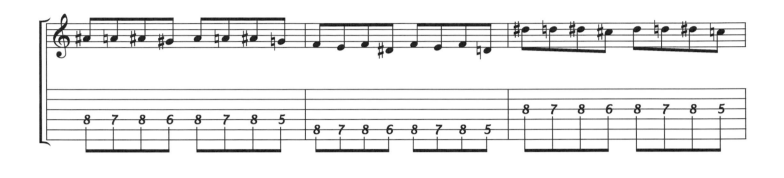

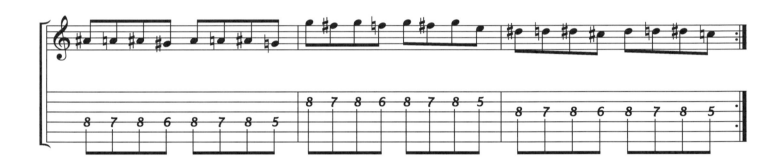

Hammer-Ons

The essence of the sound of flatpicking is to keep a precise and steady rhythm whether the note is plucked or sounded through a different technique. This exercise is crucial in improving control over the sound of hammer-ons performed with different durations.

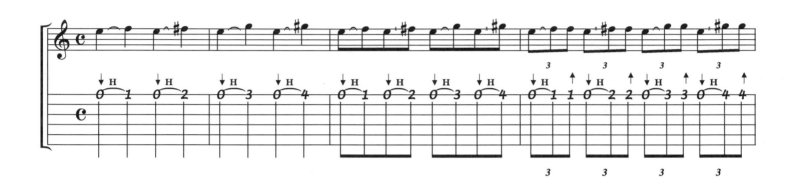

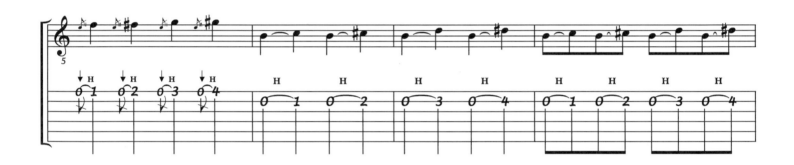

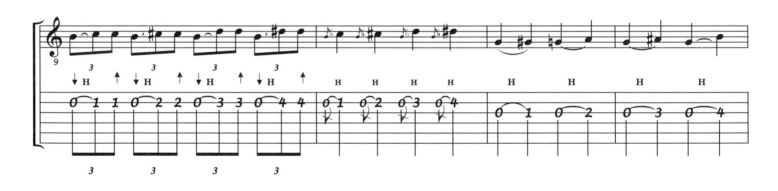

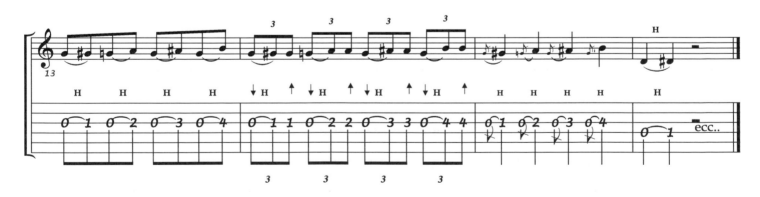

© 2010 Giuseppe Gambetta (SIAE - ITALIA)

Pull-Offs

For pull-offs, even greater attention is required. The movement needs to be carefully controlled in order to prevent the finger that produces the pull-off effect from causing the vibration of adjacent strings generating unwanted string noise.

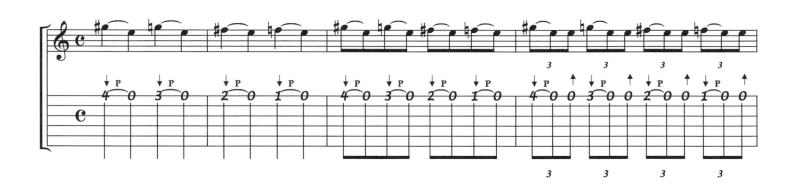

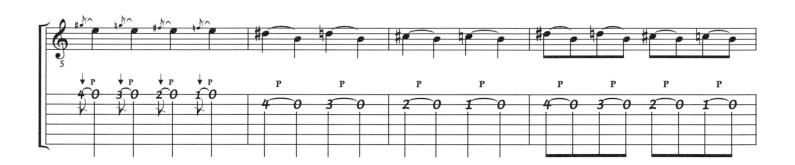

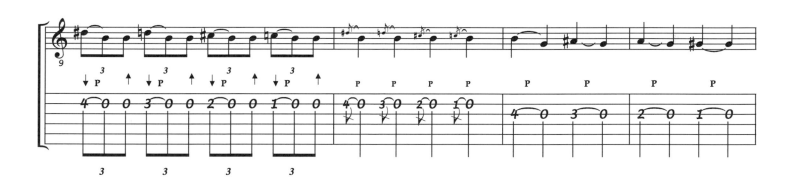

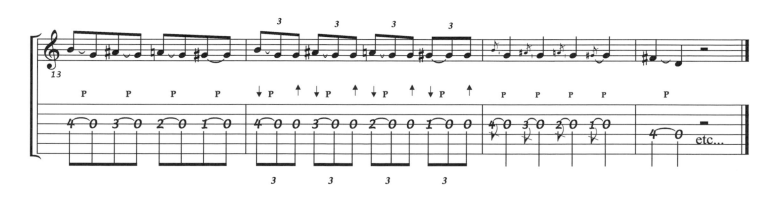

© 2010 Giuseppe Gambetta (SIAE - ITALIA)

Spider Joe (1st Pattern)

The exercise, Spider Joe, is a fingering exercise in which the left hand follows a complicated pattern that recalls the movement of a walking spider. The fingering pattern is developed on non-adjacent strings and the spider is named after the author.

© 2010 Giuseppe Gambetta (SIAE - ITALIA)

Spider Joe (2nd Pattern)

This second spider exercise can be described as a pursuit of shapes moving back and forth chromatically. The sequence is repeated and developed over non-adjacent strings.

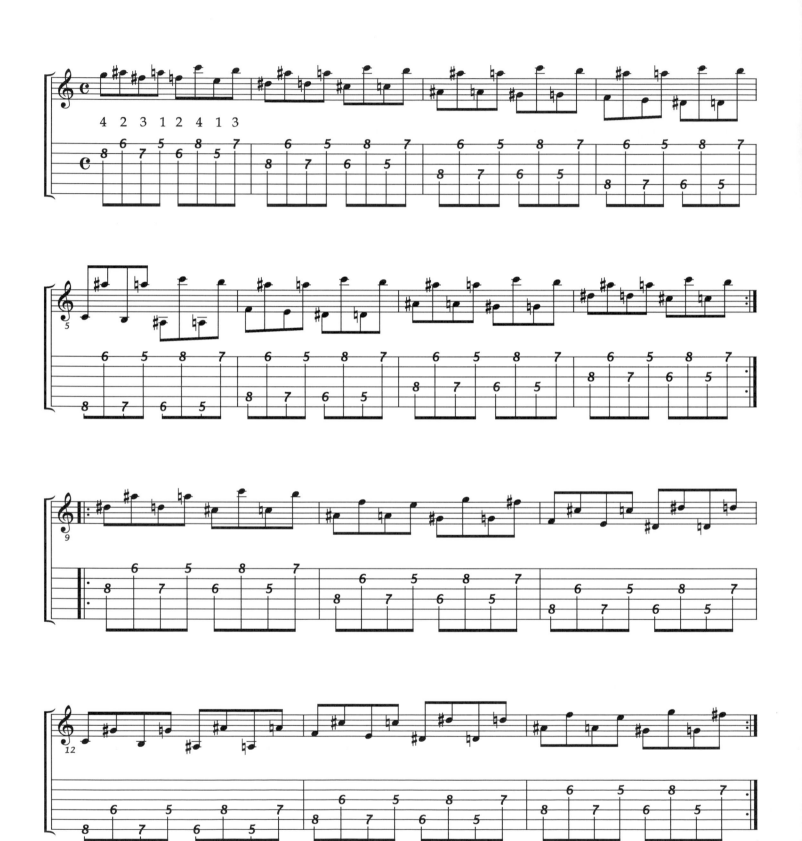

© 2010 Giuseppe Gambetta (SIAE - ITALIA)

Workout and Crosspicking

This last exercise steps up a level by combining a complicated left-hand fingering pattern with a complex *up-up, down-down* crosspicking (see crosspicking on page 51).

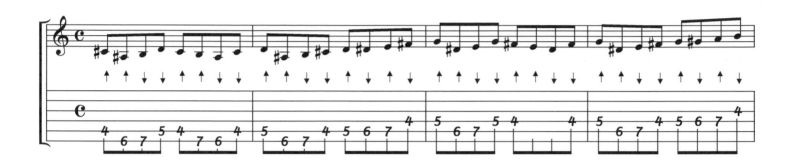

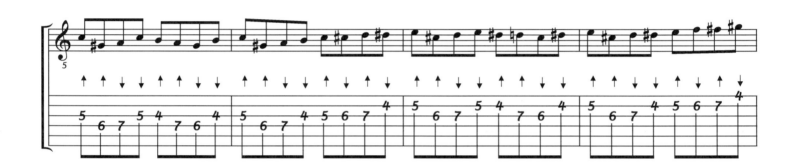

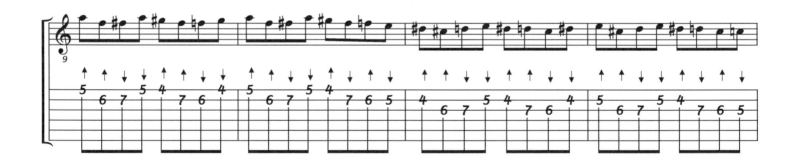

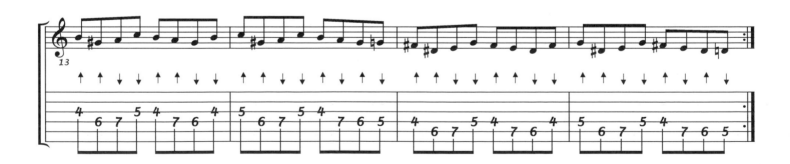

© 2010 Giuseppe Gambetta (SIAE - ITALIA)

For Beginning Students

The self-taught guitarist must avoid technical mistakes that will be hard to correct later on. The most frequent mistakes usually involve the accuracy of rhythm and timing or hand position (an incorrect placement of the thumb on the guitar neck, fingertips fretting at an incorrect angle, wrong fingering, incorrect pick grip, stiff or tentative picking and so on).

Besides focusing on playing accurately and practicing at full volume along with a metronome, it is important to have an experienced player watching and listening. Every piece of music needs to be studied in its entirety, with its harmonic progression and its accompaniment. It is very important to work on memorizing a song. The artistic and creative interpretation starts when you close the book and start playing by heart. Should a mistake occur while performing with an accompanist, most of the time it will not be necessary to stop and start over. It's better to keep playing to the end without getting out of time with the chord progression. In this way, you will learn not to lose the thread of the song; this can be very useful in understanding its structure.

However, if you make a mistake consistently, practice that phrase slowly until you can play it comfortably. The most natural approach to learning traditional music is trying to figure out the melody by ear. Part of your practice should always be dedicated to this exercise in order to improve your instinctive sensitivity to the understanding of music.

Alternate picking is the most intuitive and commonly used pick movement for playing traditional tunes.

This approach allows you to control the syncopated timing of the melody precisely and has the advantage of producing a natural emphasis on the accented beats of the measures (e.g. in 4/4 time with eighth notes accents occur on beats 1,3,5,7, which coincide with the down-stroke). It is advisable initially to practice on open strings, then move on scales or simple melodies. It is important to play along with a metronome, and to play with a full tone with quick attack and release of the string. First play *piano* (softly), then *mezzo forte* (medium) and then *forte* (loud). Experiment with different angles and pick grips.

These are the first steps for beginners. Later we will deal with the use of more complex techniques in which the pick does not follow the alternate-picking pattern but glides over the strings, picking them in the same direction.

FIRST MELODIES

The study of simple folk melodies is the first effective step towards the different styles of traditional music. Accordingly, with the approach of this book, I have chosen songs from different traditions.

These melodies are strictly related to major and minor scales and can partly replace the conventional scale practice routine.

Recommended Bibliography
Adam Granger, *Fiddle Tunes for Guitar*, Granger Publications

Recommended Recordings:
Jerry Garcia, David Grisman, *Not for Kids Only*, Acoustic Disc 1993
Beppe Gambetta, *Dialogs*, Brambus 1989

Bill Malley's Barn Dance

The first traditional tune comes from Ireland and is a further example of how the beauty of music is not necessarily related to its technical difficulty.

Traditional Irish

Rock the Cradle Joe

This tune comes from the rich American violin tradition of the Appalachian Mountains. It is played mostly with single notes but it also utilizes *double stops* (two strings played at the same time). This tune should be performed together with a second guitar playing the alternating-bass accompaniment.

Traditional American

Saltarello Romagnolo

This dance originating from northern Italy is structured in three different sections: parts A and B in the key of E minor and Part C in the key of G major. The ternary form in a 6/8 time signature raises the first technical question about the picking direction.

For this rhythm some guitarists prefer to abandon alternating picking and play the triads with a *down-down-up* movement because this pattern seems to suit the accents of the song better.

Traditional,
arranged by Beppe Gambetta

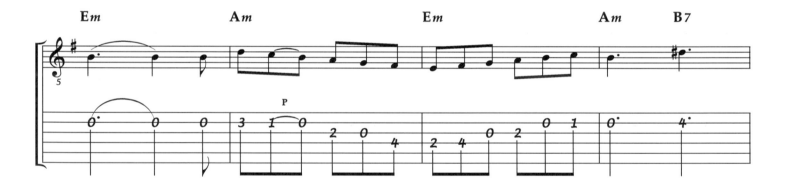

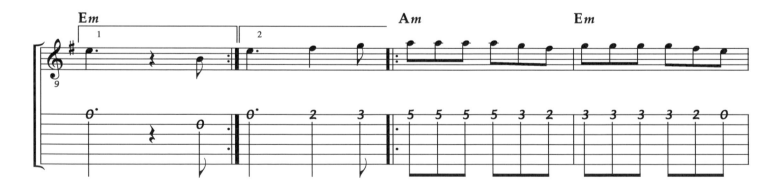

© 2010 Giuseppe Gambetta (SIAE - ITALIA)

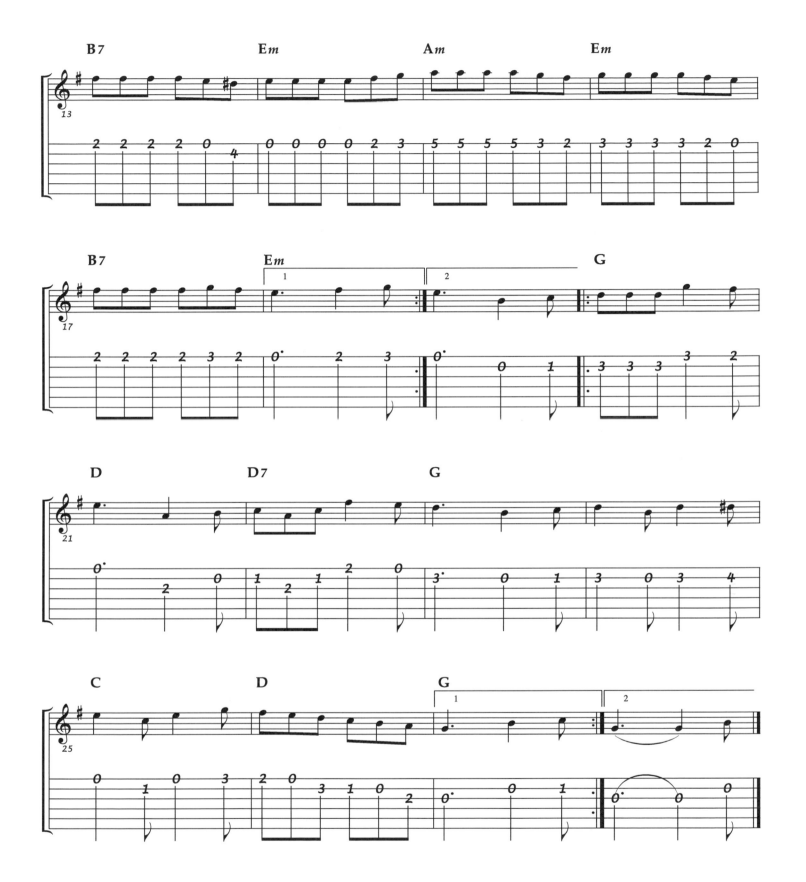

Photo by *Andrea Bosio*

Strumming

When *strumming*, the pick brushes over several strings in order to set them all in motion. It is a complex technique and represents the natural expression of flatpicking guitar. Strumming is extensively used for various functions ranging from rhythm guitar to soloing. It should be studied in all its forms and nuances, which sometimes require careful control.

Strumming is rarely performed freely on all six strings. Sometimes a specific note needs to be highlighted and other times it should be performed with a muted effect or with a percussive sound. Finally, it is sometimes preferable to mute the strings just after they have been played. Be prepared to constantly switch the set of strings to be played, together with the intensity, the speed and the strumming pattern.

All of these are the fundamental elements on which this comprehensive exercise is based.

The arrangements of the following tunes is designed to highlight the usage of strumming both with a chordal and a melodic emphasis. It is possible to highlight the last strummed note by resting the pick on the next string not being played. This way the accompaniment chords and the highlighted notes of the melody sound simultaneously.

5

Down in the Valley to Pray

The first song that I have arranged is traditional gospel, handed down by Doc Watson. There have been many outstanding vocal versions, but it really seems to be made for guitar strumming. The arrangement uses a first alteration of standard tuning by lowering the sixth string to D (drop D tuning).

Tuning: D A D G B E
Capo on the 2nd fret

Traditional

Geordie

This is the melody of an anonymous English ballad. It is popular thanks to the Italian version by Fabrizio De Andrè, and it works well as an instrumental piece when strummed. For those who sing the song this part can be used as a solo between verses.

Traditional

Sally Goodin

In this very popular American fiddle tune, I purposely varied the placement of the accents and alternated the strumming between the downbeats and the upbeats of the measure. This offers an example of the variations that may arise from a creative strumming approach.

Traditional,
arranged by Beppe Gambetta

Tuning: D A D G B E

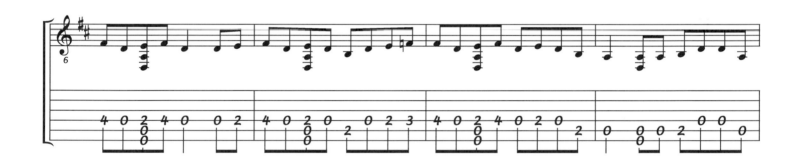

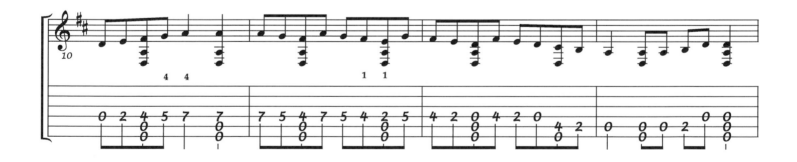

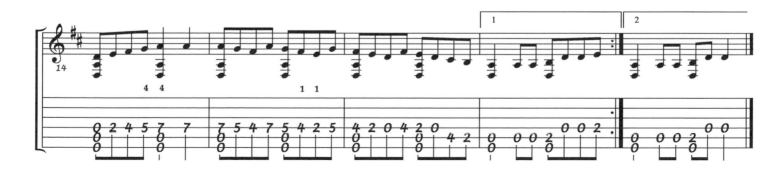

© 2010 Giuseppe Gambetta (SIAE - ITALIA)

Cuckoo's Nest

This song in drop D tuning comes from the American traditional repertoire. The arrangement has been enriched with embellishments and variations, and is technically more difficult than the previous songs.

Traditional,
arranged by Beppe Gambetta

Tuning: D A D G B E

© 2010 Giuseppe Gambetta (SIAE - ITALIA)

Photo by *Simon Anhorn*

Accompaniment

As earlier mentioned, the popular guitar was traditionally used as an accompanying instrument. In this role it expresses a fundamental part of its character, acting as an artistic engine and playing a versatile and creative role in the composition of melodies and songs. Contemporary audiences often exalt the role of the soloist, while not paying as much attention to the beauty and the artistic importance of accompanying rhythmic support. Being based on the repetition of a simple and familiar pattern, rhythm exercises are often considered unappealing.

The accompaniment, however, is an art form of an especially skilled simplicity that only few can master to perfection, supporting the rhythm of songs and music compositions in a dynamic and creative way. This is a very important topic as it represents 90% of the work done by the guitar when playing in a band. It is often an intricate task, aimed not only at providing the rhythm for the band but also at building the back-up, in order to highlight the voices and create space for vocals and instruments as they alternate in the foreground.

Accompaniment should therefore not be underestimated and should be carefully exercised in all of its nuances and dynamics.

When playing a rhythm with alternating bass, the bass line must be precise and powerful. The strumming on the highest strings needs to be fast and light so as to avoid overpowering the bass. Upstrokes, in particular, should be very delicate and are often played only on the first string in order to emphasize its lightness.

Some artists poetically suggest that you imagine having a wet hand shaking off water drops while practicing. The most common instinctive mistake is a tendency to increase the pace when playing at high volume and slowing down when playing at low volume. It is imperative to practice with a metronome in order to get used to varying the volume at any time and without affecting the timing.

Recommended Bibliography:
Happy Traum, *Bluegrass Guitar*, Oak Publications 1974
Fred Sokolow, *Strum & Picking Patterns*, Hal Leonard 1995
Jerry Silverman, *The Folk Singer's Guitar Guide*, Oak Publications 1964

Recommended Recordings:
Doc & Merle Watson, *Down South*, Sugar Hill 1984
The Nashville Bluegrass Band, *The Boys are Back in Town*, Sugar Hill 1990
Hot Rize, *So Long of a Journey*, Sugar Hill 2002
Guy Clark, *The Dark*, Sugar Hill 2002

Alternating Bass Rhythms

The first five examples show the most common alternating bass-rhythm patterns based on a simple chord progression. The following three show a more complex pattern of treble notes in-between. The sequence ends with three examples of various feels (with no alternating bass), showing how acoustic guitar rhythm can adjust to fit different styles.

© 2010 Giuseppe Gambetta (SIAE - ITALIA)

Alternating Bass Rhythms

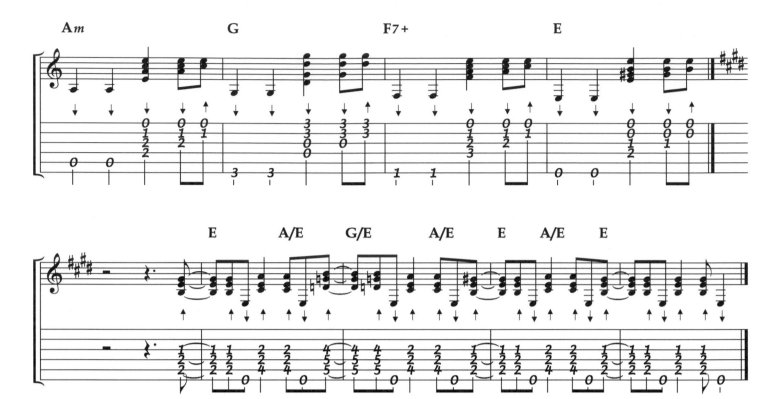

Rhythm and Strumming

Rhythms without alternating bass work differently as the interplay of accents on groups of higher or lower strings generate the dynamics and the contrasts that define the rhythm.

The rhythmic movement of the right hand must be fluid and free. It partially involves the arm but fundamentally it is obtained with a partial rotatory motion of the wrist.

The examples refer to sonorities that gradually turn away from the world of folk tradition. The final three examples involve swing, muted strumming, and reggae.

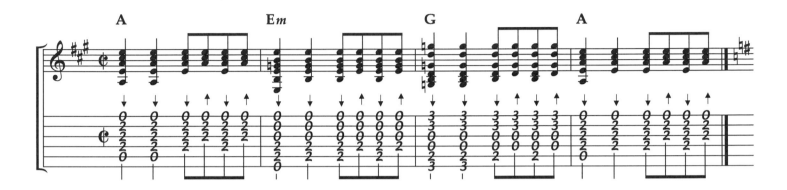

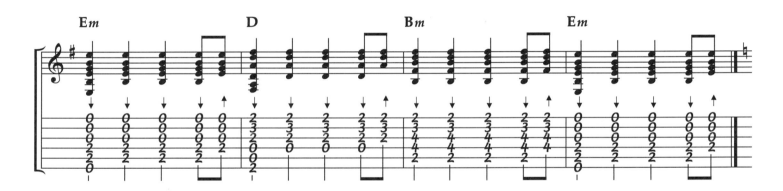

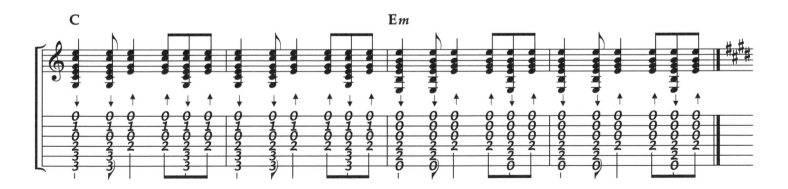

© 2010 Giuseppe Gambetta (SIAE - ITALIA)

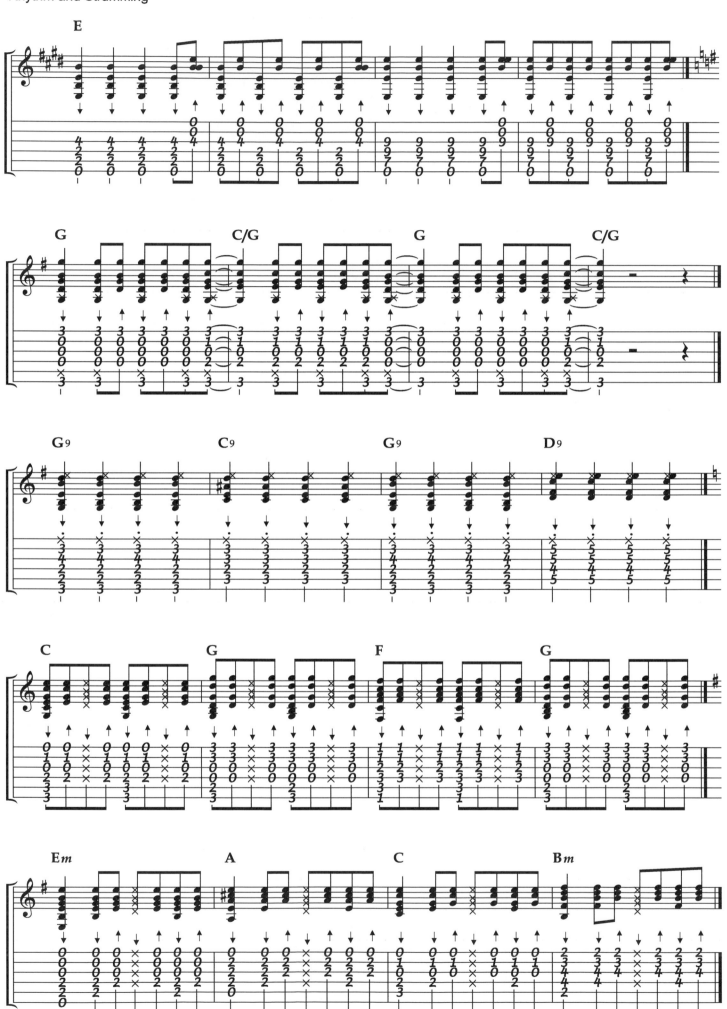

Fill-in Licks

It is difficult to define precisely what a guitar can accomplish beyond "standard" movements. Bass lines and transitions, bass runs and fill-in licks should be balanced with taste. Difficulties may arise from the simplicity and repetitiveness of the harmonic progression in some songs. The issue of originality concerns, in particular, the bass notes, which highlight chord changes with lines that connect the different harmonies.

To give you an idea you can vary the bass line by playing the notes with different durations or by playing in half, quarter or eighth notes. You could also choose to play on the back-beat or decide not to play the bass note where it would be more obvious to do so. Bass lines can also be changed by varying the number of notes to be played (from one to four or more notes in the musical phrase).

The major technical difficulty of the back-up concerns the right hand, which must limit the free rhythmic movement at the proper time to concentrate on playing the phrases. The following examples show some of these phrases which, in order to fit into the gaps in the melodic line, are typically very short. In American slang they are called *fill-in licks*.

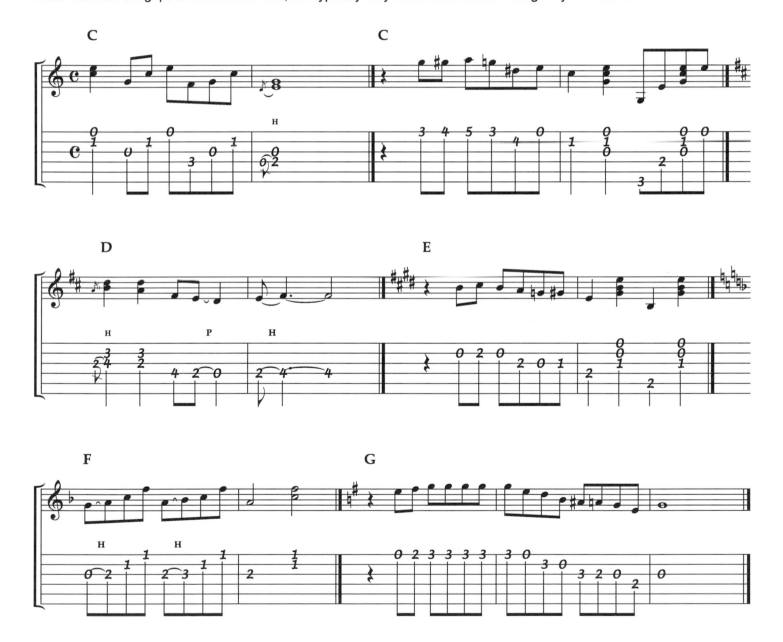

© 2010 Giuseppe Gambetta (SIAE - ITALIA)

Bass Runs

Among the fill-in phrases, the so-called bass runs stand out. Bass runs are phrases built mainly on the lower registers of the instrument. They refine the sound with a solid presence. The following examples are in different keys.

The examples in the key of G are variations of the traditional G run, a phrasing created at the dawn of Bluegrass music by the legendary guitarist Lester Flatt, and has become a cliché of this music.

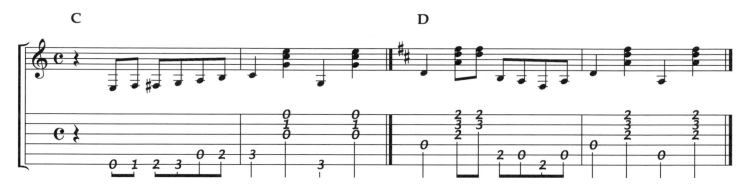

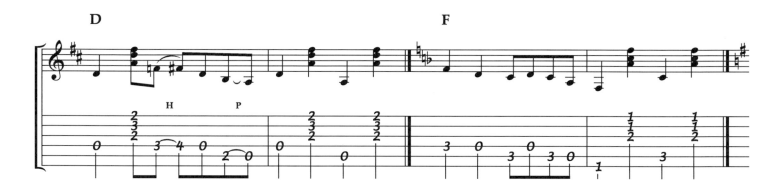

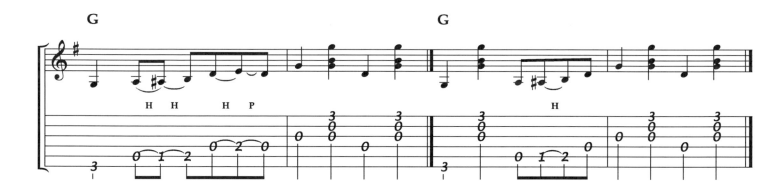

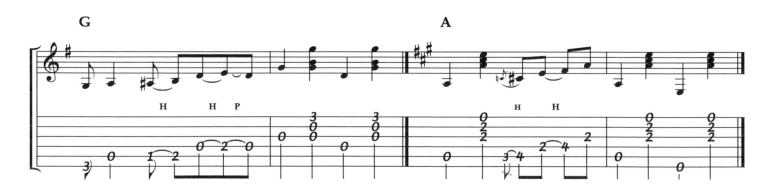

© 2010 Giuseppe Gambetta (SIAE - ITALIA)

Rhythm Licks

Rhythm licks do not have the function of response and refinement. They form a steady rhythmic foundation on which to build the structure of the arrangement. Some of the examples approach electric rock-blues-country. It is very entertaining to improvise and create the sound of a song by coordinating and overlapping these moves with those of a second strumming guitar.

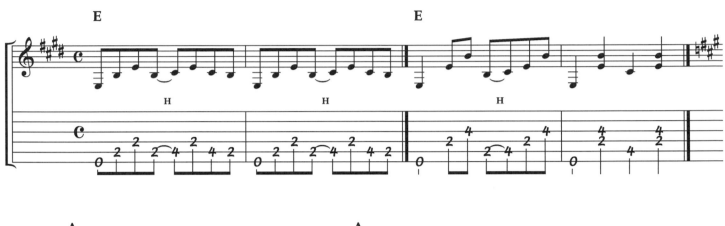

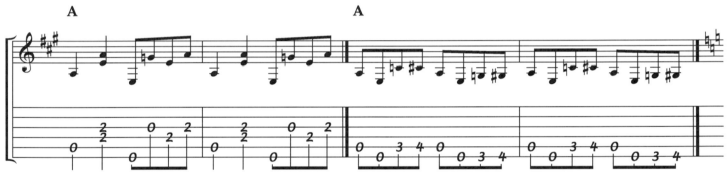

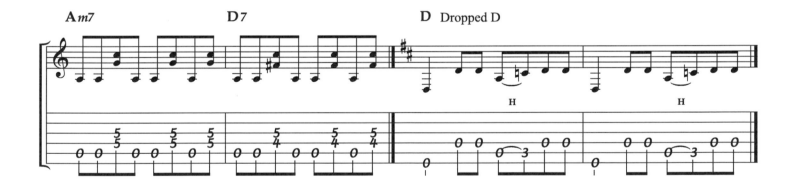

© 2010 Giuseppe Gambetta (SIAE - ITALIA)

Photo by *Federica Calvino Prina*

Carter Style

The Carter Style technique is named after the very popular band that enjoyed great popularity across the United States in the '30s, a time of increasingly widespread radio broadcast. The Carter Family came from WestVirginia and was formed by Alvin Pleasant, his wife Sarah and his sister-in-law Maybelle.

It was Maybelle's guitar that characterized the band's sound with a solo technique based on a melodic line played on the lowest strings leaving the strumming of the accompaniment unchanged in the spaces within the melodic line.

The Carter Style is the perfect synthesis of history and technique. A style that belongs to the past and, at the same time, represents a comprehensive and balanced exercise for the approach to flatpicking guitar. It develops an instinctive understanding of the relationship between melody and harmony and, even today, is applied by contemporary artists to various styles.

Despite the apparent simplicity, it is rather difficult to play the Carter Style well, especially from a rhythmic and dynamic point of view. The notes of the melody must stand out with a stronger presence than the rest and must be performed with great rhythmic fluidity.

Limited space is left for variations and embellishments, as the left hand is mainly anchored to the chord positions. Simple variations based on pull-offs and hammer-ons can be included.

"Lonesome Road Blues" is a traditional, classic 'white' blues and is an excellent example of the Carter Style. As in some other songs included in this book, the first chorus presents the melody in its essential form whereas the second introduces the first arpeggios and a few variations.

"Gentleman Charlie" is an example of a modern composition inspired by old styles. It is from my "Slade Stomp" CD and is dedicated to Charlie Waller, a guitarist of the early days of Bluegrass who used to play with the "Country Gentlemen".

The sound is developed on a base traditionally very close to the Carter Style with the addition of some refined embellishments. When approaching the study of this song, attention must be paid to the strums —which are all "short" (played on two strings only). Take care on the two string *down-down-up* crosspicking that, when played as a fast triplet, generates a sort of a trill effect (see bars 5, 13, 24, 30, 31).

Recommended Bibliography:
Mark Zwonitzer, Charles Hirshberg, *Will you miss me when I'm gone?*, Simon & Schuster 2002

Recommended Recordings:
The Carter Family, *Worried Man Blues*, Rounder 1995
Delmore Brothers, *Brown's Ferry Blues*, County Records, 1995
Nick Lucas, *Painting the clouds*, Soundies
The New Lost City Ramblers, *The Early Years*,
Smithsonian/Folkways Records 1991

Lonesome Road Blues

Traditional,
arranged by Beppe Gambetta

Capo on the 2nd fret

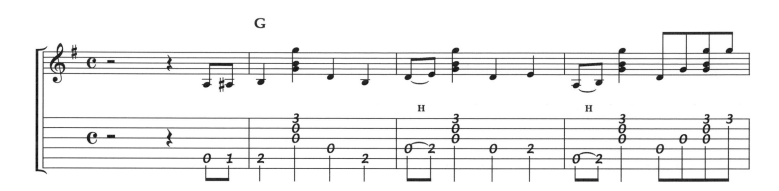

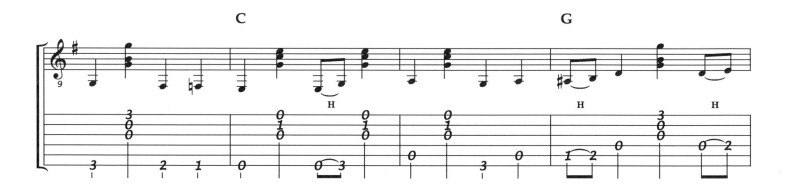

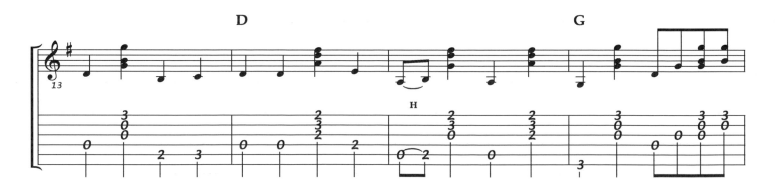

© 2010 Giuseppe Gambetta (SIAE - ITALIA)

Gentleman Charlie

Beppe Gambetta

© 2010 Giuseppe Gambetta (SIAE - ITALIA)

The examples that I have chosen are a first step towards mastering this style and will also lead to an instinctive understanding of it without the need to consult sheet music.

Try to perform a familiar tune in the Carter Style. You might try "This Land Is Your Land" and "Blowing in the Wind", for example, or other simple diatonic tune.

Crosspicking

Crosspicking is a complex and creative technique that has its origin in American traditional flatpicking. It is also found with different characteristics, in many other traditions, and more recently, it has generated interesting experimental innovations in the world of stringed instruments.

The term *crosspicking* indicates arpeggios played with a pick on adjacent strings, the result of plucking multiple strings in the same direction. These patterns of arpeggios can be applied to various situations: they can highlight melodic lines or simply function as accompaniment.

What makes the sound of this style so interesting is the use of the *rest stroke* technique (the pick rests on the next string before picking it). This creates brightness and rhythm, and the placement of odd accents against a steady beat often generates interesting contrasts.

For some purists, the term *crosspicking* only indicates the traditional movements played across three strings, as developed in the American tradition. In order to simplify, in this book we will use this term for similar styles borrowed from other traditions as well.

Seen from a broader perspective, crosspicking is not only used in the Doc Watson fiddle tunes, but can be found in some cascading licks by Django Reinhardt, in the embellishments of Celtic guitar, in the strumming that accompanies the Sardinian dances of Logudoro or in the Cuban technique of plucking stringed instruments. The list of examples from different cultures is surprisingly varied.

Complex studies of this technique have been carried out, in the field of electric jazz-guitar, by artists like Frank Gambale. Compared to these insights, the traditional acoustic approach focuses mostly on the use of open strings or groups of strings and rhythmic patterns related to popular dance music.

ESSENTIAL MOVEMENTS

These first patterns form the basic movements to be repeated patiently as a preparatory crosspicking exercise. Follow the picking direction carefully as indicated in the score, and "rest" the pick on the next string when the movement continues in the same direction.

I would recommend the following seven exercises: The first two (*down-down-up* and *up-up-down*) are the most traditional. They can be heard in the repertoire of Doc Watson, George Shuffler and other traditional American masters and are played across three adjacent strings.

The third and fourth example show the most advanced expression of the same pattern: *down-down-up* and *up-up-down* on two adjacent strings, plucking the second string one more time. The *down-down-up* pattern is already present in Django Reinhardt's *manouche* style and it is developed by Brad Davis and other, more progressive, American guitarists. Among other things, it allows you to create incredibly fast hot licks (see *down-down-up* licks on page 115 and 116).

The last three examples refer to "crossed" crosspicking (the two directions are alternated) played on three, four and five strings.

Crosspicking Fundamentals

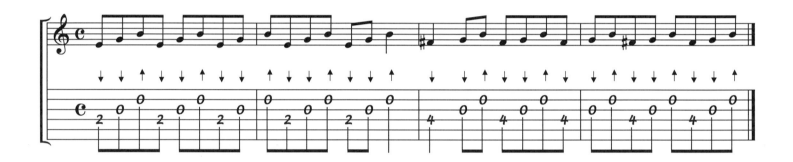

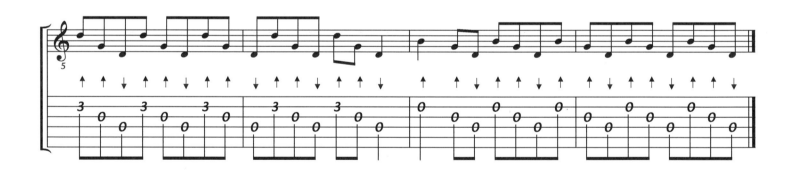

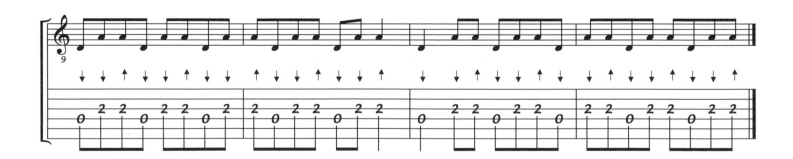

© 2010 Giuseppe Gambetta (SIAE - ITALIA)

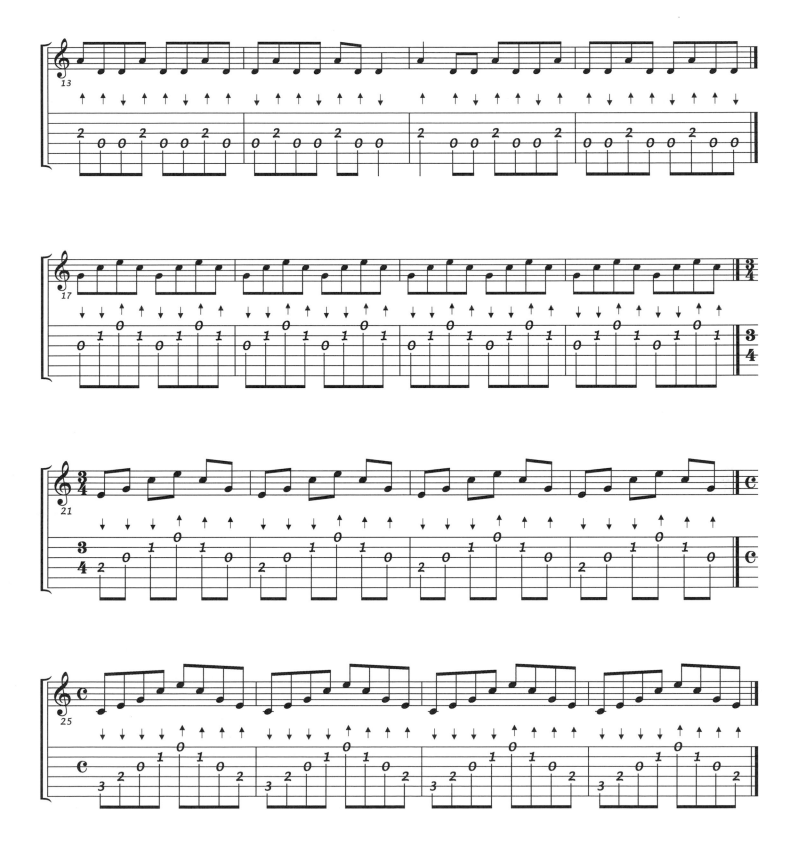

ARRANGING A TRADITIONAL MELODY WITH CROSSPICKING

Looking more closely, in this arrangement of "The Banks of the Ohio" there are *down-down-up* or *up-up-down* patterns played on two or three strings with pull-offs and hammer-ons now and then to create variations to interrupt boring repetitions.

In the second progression, where difficulty increases, effects and variations are more frequent. After a short initial stage, necessary to understand the melody, the study needs to be focused on the correct picking direction as shown on the tabs, as this is the main aim of teaching the arrangement (naturally, down arrows stand for down strokes while up arrows stand for up strokes). If you experience difficulty learning the exact movement, stay on each bar or phrase, repeating over and over short musical fragments before joining them together.

Once this skill is properly achieved, you can improve the technique by by accentuating the melodic notes and de-emphasizing the fill-in notes of the arpeggio.

"The Banks of the Ohio" is a well-known traditional ballad about a man in love who kills the woman who rejected him. While singing the song, these parts can be used as an introduction, or as a solo between the different verses.

The Banks of the Ohio

Traditional,

arranged by Beppe Gambetta

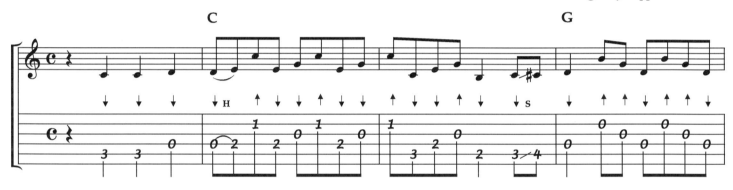

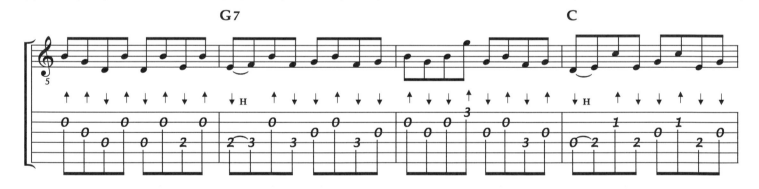

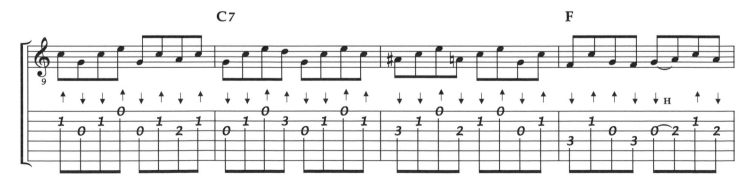

© 2010 Giuseppe Gambetta (SIAE - ITALIA)

Arkansas Traveller

In the crosspicking version of "Arkansas Traveller" (a traditional dance performed, in the old time versions, interchanging the music with a comedic conversation between the farmer and the wayfarer) technical difficulties, similar to those of the previous track, can be found, but with the addition of different kinds of alternating arpeggios, often involving more than the traditional three strings.

Traditional,
arranged by Beppe Gambetta

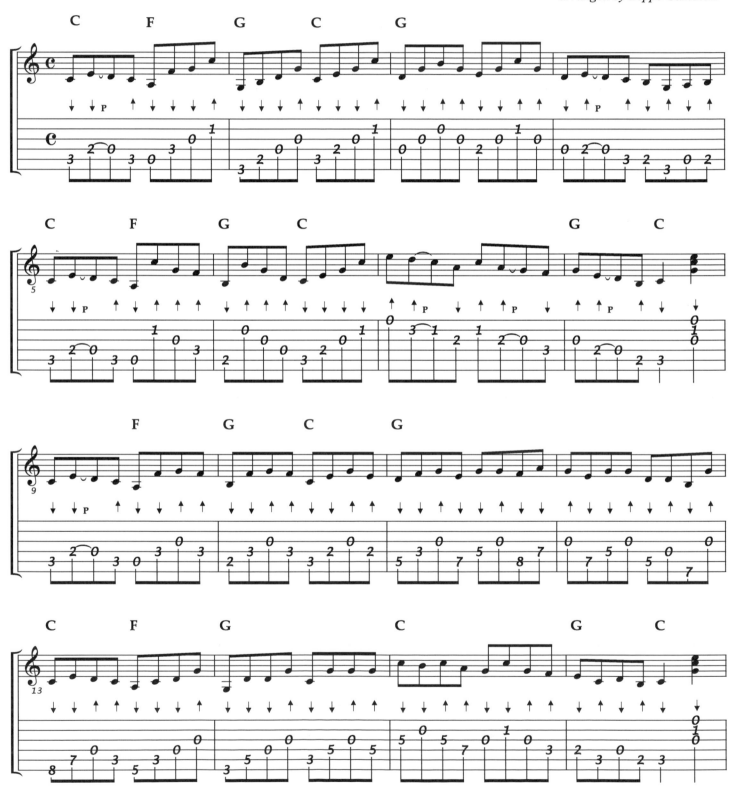

© 2010 Giuseppe Gambetta (SIAE - ITALIA)

Crosspicking: Creative Examples

The following examples show creative crosspicking solutions in different situations, not necessarily related to a soloing context. The different examples involve rhythmic patterns, textures, drones and the creation of triplets.

These are just a few ideas for using crosspicking in different contexts.

The most complex piece of music in which I have developed an integration of different kinds of tremolo is my transcription of the traditional Sardinian Ave Maria, "Deus Ti Salvet Maria" (see page 144).

Rhythmic Groove

Beppe Gambetta

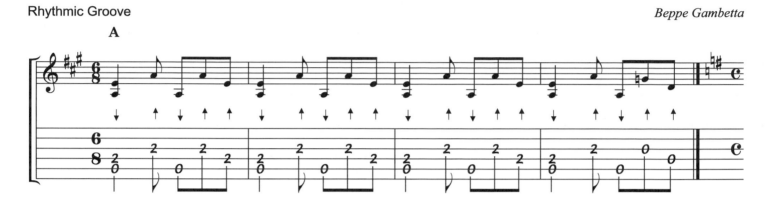

Triplets

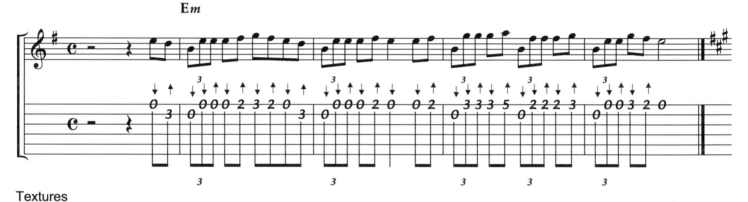

Textures

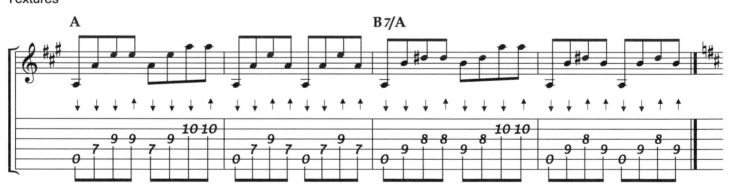

Drones (on lower strings)

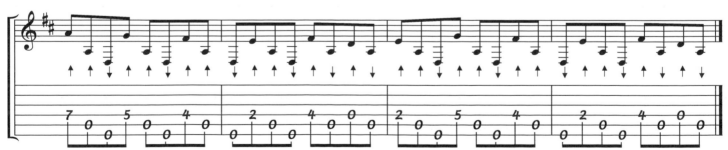

© 2010 Giuseppe Gambetta (SIAE - ITALIA)

Sardinian Crosspicking

The musical form of the Sardinian guitar dance developed mainly in the Logudoro region (located in the north-west area of the island). It is characterized by the performance of three alternating singers, accompanied by a guitar and often by an accordion as well. During the concerts, called *gare* (contests), the guitar has a primarily accompanying role. But, in the spaces between the performances of the different singers, it plays small solos in which sophisticated techniques and riveting sonorities emerge.

It is interesting to note that, for this flatpicking style, a uniquely indigenous kind of guitar has been developed, similar to a baritone guitar, tuned down two or three whole steps. We do not know exactly who pioneered this style but the most acknowledged names are Nicolino Cabitza, Aldo Cabitza and Adolfo Merella. At present, the most important active guitarist is Tore Matzau. Apart from this traditional school there are several guitarists who are inspired by the Sardinian tradition, although they are devoted to contemporary music. This tradition originates as guitar music and cannot be considered a revival, since it is still alive and widely practiced. This guitar technique is absolutely original and totally refers to the technique of crosspicking on groups of multiple strings. It is based on repetitive movements with rhythmic variations and chord changes, sometimes obtained by inserting single-note scales. Here are some of the most common variations. The first six bars simply represent the intro to the song, with a few chords played on the downbeat. Bars 7 to 12 are examples of a typical dance movement where the guitar remains on a D chord and the main difficulty is to control down-strokes by dividing the movement into two parts: first the fourth, third and second string together, and, after a short rest, the first string alone, and finally, only the first string with an upstroke.

Finally, in bars 13-18, another fundamental pattern is presented, passing alternatively from a D to an A7 chord. This pattern is very similar to the previous one, but it is built on a different number of strings (two at a time) over which the pick glides, playing in the same direction.

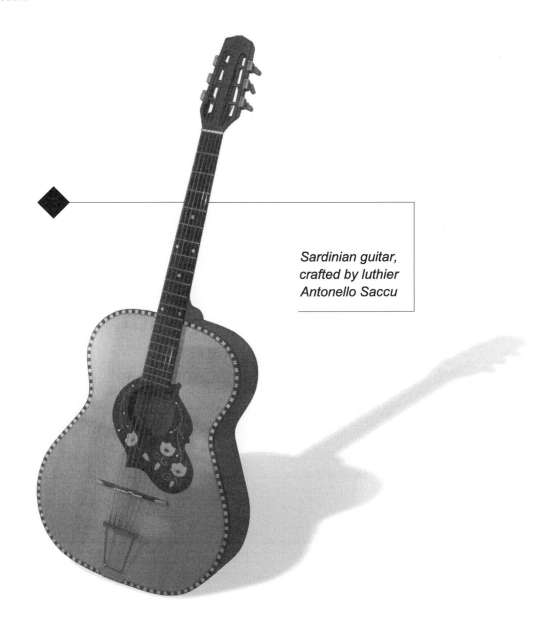

Sardinian guitar, crafted by luthier Antonello Saccu

Ballo a Chitarra (Guitar Dance)

Traditional Sardinian Dance

Transcription and Rearrangement of Traditional Melodies

9

The burgeoning development of flatpicking styles owes no small part to the transcription of traditional melodies. Studying such transcriptions is a crucial step towards improving technical skills.

For those at a more advanced level, searching for and transcribing new songs that lend themselves to flatpicking guitar is both fun and a vital part of keeping this acoustic guitar technique alive.

It is certainly essential to preserve and pass on traditional songs, which have sometimes been forgotten, or were played by instruments that are no longer popular.

The choice of a traditional song that lends itself to acoustic guitar repertoire is not always obvious: you often have to listen to and try out different songs at length before you can home in on a song fit for transcription. Sometimes the work becomes more artistically creative and more rewarding when the song is rearranged with substantial changes such as key, tempo, and reworking parts of the melody to make it more suitable for the technique used. In most cases, this work requires an effort in terms of creativity and artistic sensibility, approaching the level of skill and dedication required for composing.

THE REPERTOIRE OF AMERICAN FIDDLE TUNES

THE REPERTOIRE OF AMERICAN FIDDLE TUNES
The old-time American dance tunes are often called "Fiddle Tunes" because they are associated with the repertoire of traditional violin. These represent the vast source from which Doc Watson drew to develop the flatpicking guitar repertoire.

Some of these melodies have become must-know standards for musicians playing at jam sessions that originate spontaneously all over the world as meeting points for enthusiastic flatpickers.

Most of this repertoire has flourished in the Appalachian Mountains where melodies of European origin (Irish in particular) have evolved, altered and formed a melting pot of different ethnicities, influenced also by Afro-American components. These tunes have developed into a very interesting repertoire, particularly suitable to the acoustic guitar, for which it represents a fundamental transitional experience. It is interesting to study the creative ideas of the different performers: the tendency to stick to the melody on the one hand and to create daring variations on the other.

Kitchen Girl

Traditional,
arranged by Beppe Gambetta

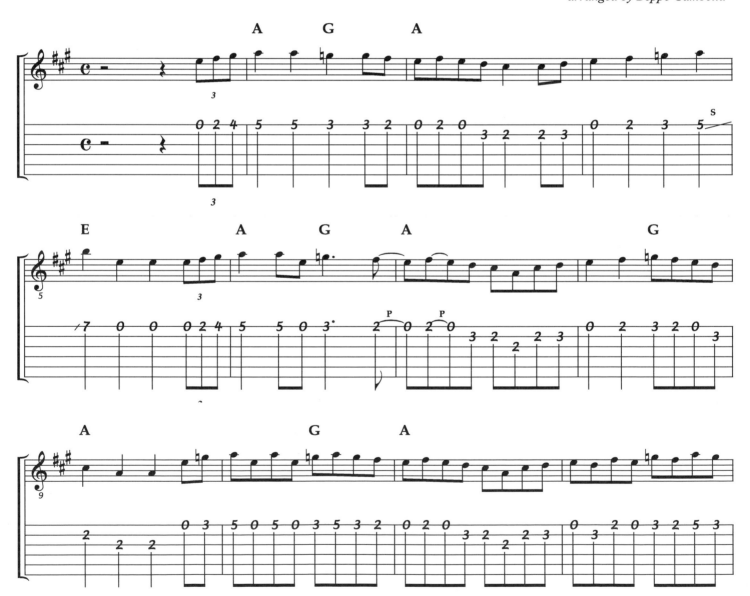

© 2010 Giuseppe Gambetta (SIAE - ITALIA)

Blackberry Blossom

Traditional,
arranged by Beppe Gambetta

© 2010 Giuseppe Gambetta (SIAE - ITALIA)

Blackberry Blossom
(Variations)

Traditional,
variations by Beppe Gambetta

© 2010 Giuseppe Gambetta (SIAE - ITALIA)

EASTERN EUROPEAN TRADITIONAL MELODIES

One of the most rewarding aspects of my job as a musician is to familiarize myself with the music and musicians from far away countries. In Europe, Balkan music is certainly an infinite source of beautiful melodies. This is an example of the music I heard in Moravia, a region in the Czech Republic and a land of multiple ethnic and cultural boundaries, where the cross pollination of the "cultured" heritage with the "Gypsy" tradition creates great effective synergies.On the guitar, the most entertaining approach was to transpose and rearrange the complicated traditional violin melodies, trying to keep the rhythmic intensity intact by exploiting the vigorous timing of the flatpicking technique and using it to reproduce the dynamic accelerations typical of that tradition.

Czardas

Traditional Hungarian dance,
arranged by Beppe Gambetta

© 2010 Giuseppe Gambetta (SIAE - ITALIA)

VARIOUS TRADITIONAL ITALIAN MELODIES

The following transcriptions show a wide variety of musical styles from different Italian regions. These are just a small sample of a vast repertoire that is waiting to be rediscovered and revisited on the acoustic guitar.

The first piece is an Emilian dance. It comes from the traditional violin repertoire, handed down to the present day by the legendary senior violinist Melchiade Benni. Many of its parts are perfectly suitable to be played with the crosspicking technique, evidencing certain aesthetic similarities.

The second piece, on the other hand, is a suite of polkas and quadrilles from Puglia (already recorded on my "Slade Stomp" CD).

The quadrille is a historic dance performed by four couples in a rectangular formation, and a precursor to traditional square dancing. It is also a style of music. The suite is taken from the traditional mandolin repertoire handed down by barbers and has been transcribed with the embellishments and variations on an imaginary continuation of the Italian folk-guitar style. The accompaniment and bass lines are not simple so I decided to publish the entire transcription of that part too.

Bergamasca

Traditional Italian Dance,
arranged by Beppe Gambetta

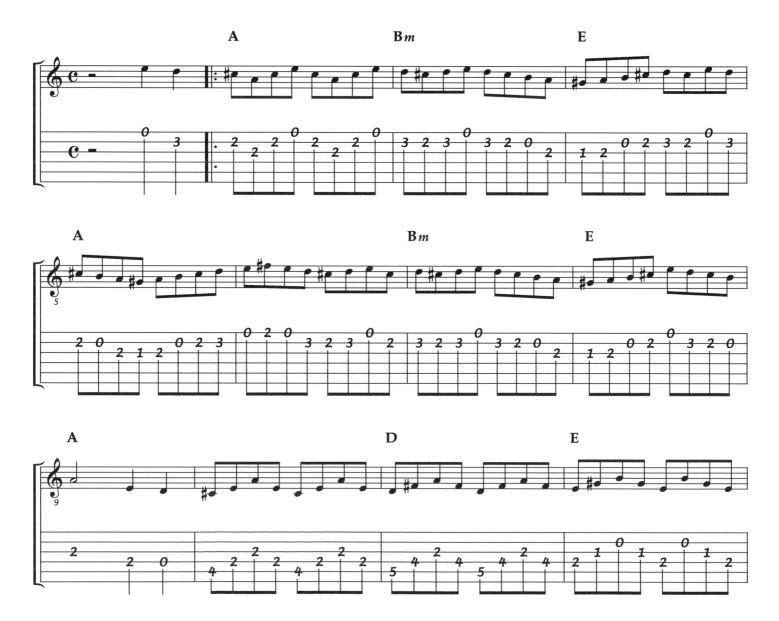

© 2010 Giuseppe Gambetta (SIAE - ITALIA)

Bergamasca

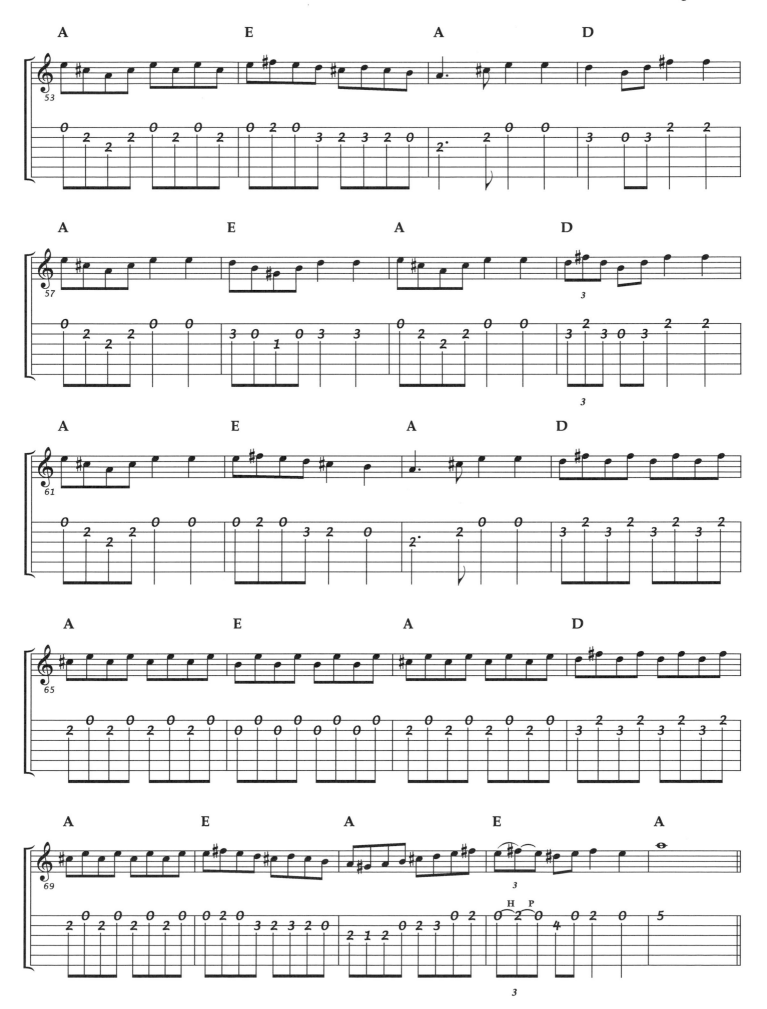

Suite of Polkas and Quadrilles

Traditional Italian Dances,
arranged by Beppe Gambetta

© 2010 Giuseppe Gambetta (SIAE - ITALIA)

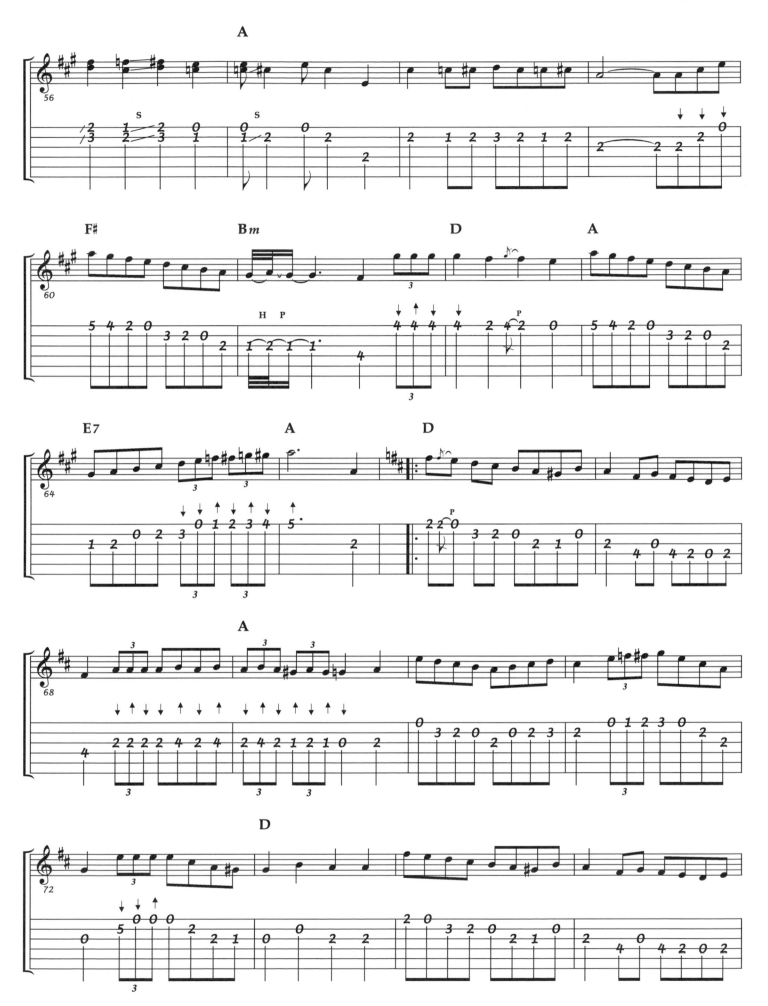

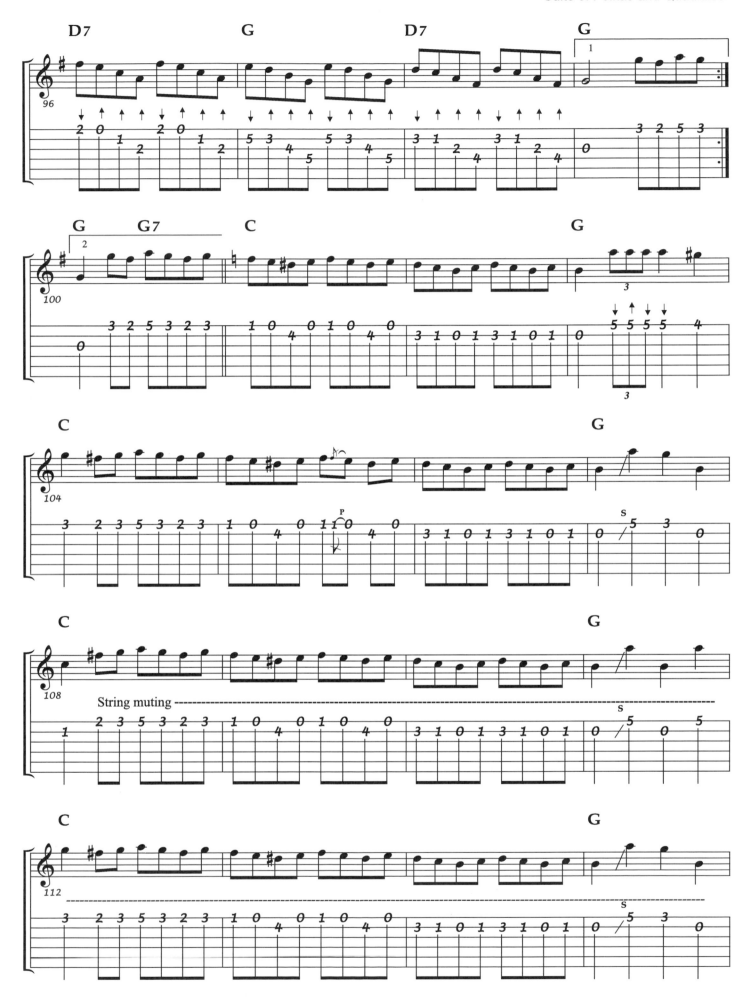

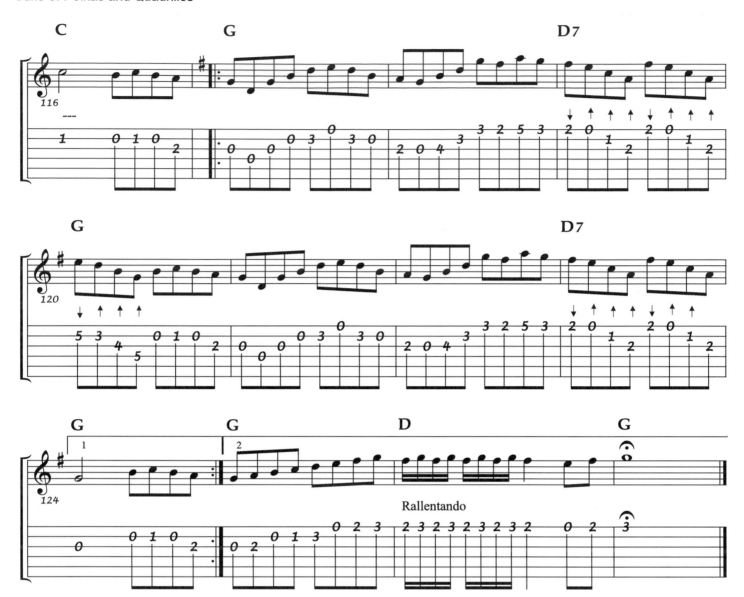

Suite of Polkas and Quadrilles
(Accompaniment)

Traditional Italian Dances,
arranged by Beppe Gambetta

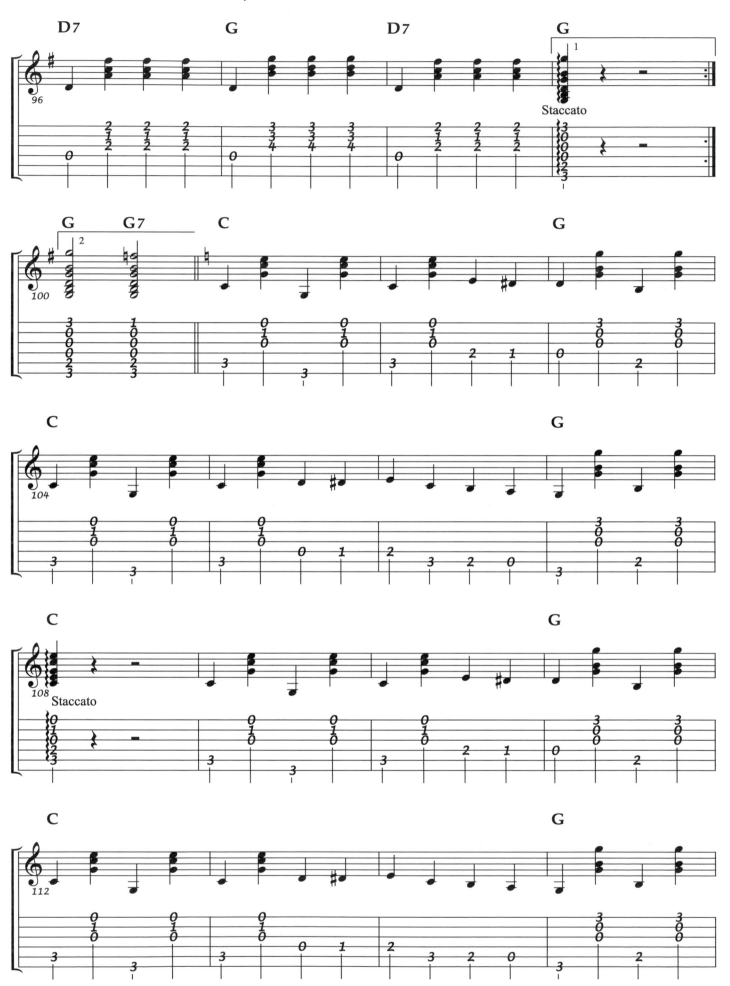

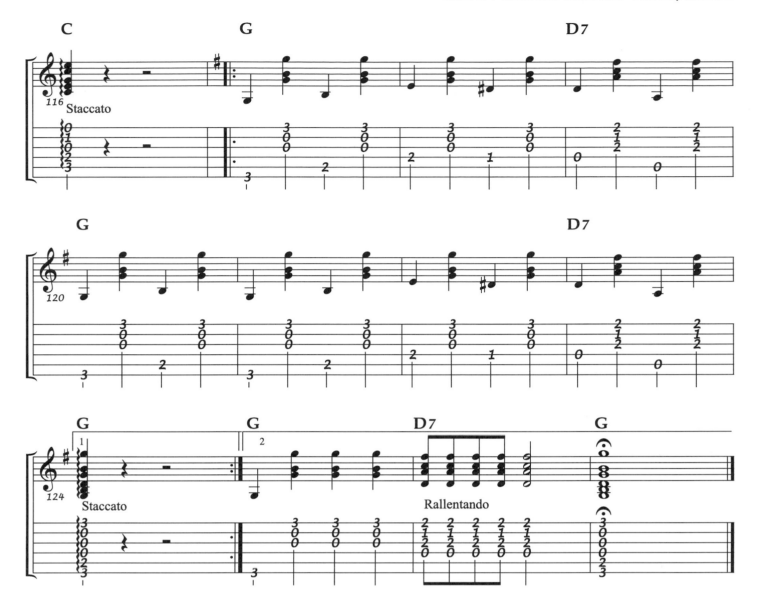

FLATPICKING IN THE BRITISH ISLES

In the musical tradition of the British Isles, referring mainly to Ireland and Scotland, the guitar was not taken into consideration until the folk revival of the '60s. As with all popular evolution, the guitar was initially played as a rhythm instrument and only later was its melodic potential developed by more advanced artists.
One one hand the absence of a precise and codified style created difficulties; on the other it gave guitarists immense opportunities to experiment with new solutions.
The biggest challenge was to arrange the pipe tunes for guitar and, in particular, to arrange them for flatpicking techniques.

In 1977 the Scottish artist Dick Gaughan recorded an album entirely of guitar music: "Coppers and Brass", which was a synthesis of his research on traditional material. Among the Scottish guitar fathers the legendary "Peerie" Willie Johnson from Shetland is worth remembering. As a young man he emigrated to the U.S. where he met Eddie Lang, the father of swing guitar. Upon his return to his native islands, Willie began to accompany the local violinists thus becoming, unintentionally, the founder of the Shetland guitar style.

Coleraine

Irish Jig,
arranged by Beppe Gambetta

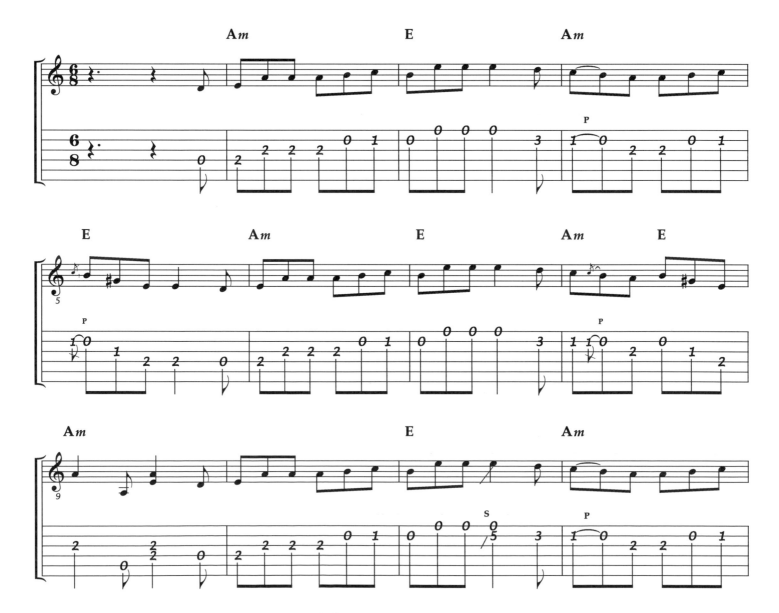

© 2010 Giuseppe Gambetta (SIAE - ITALIA)

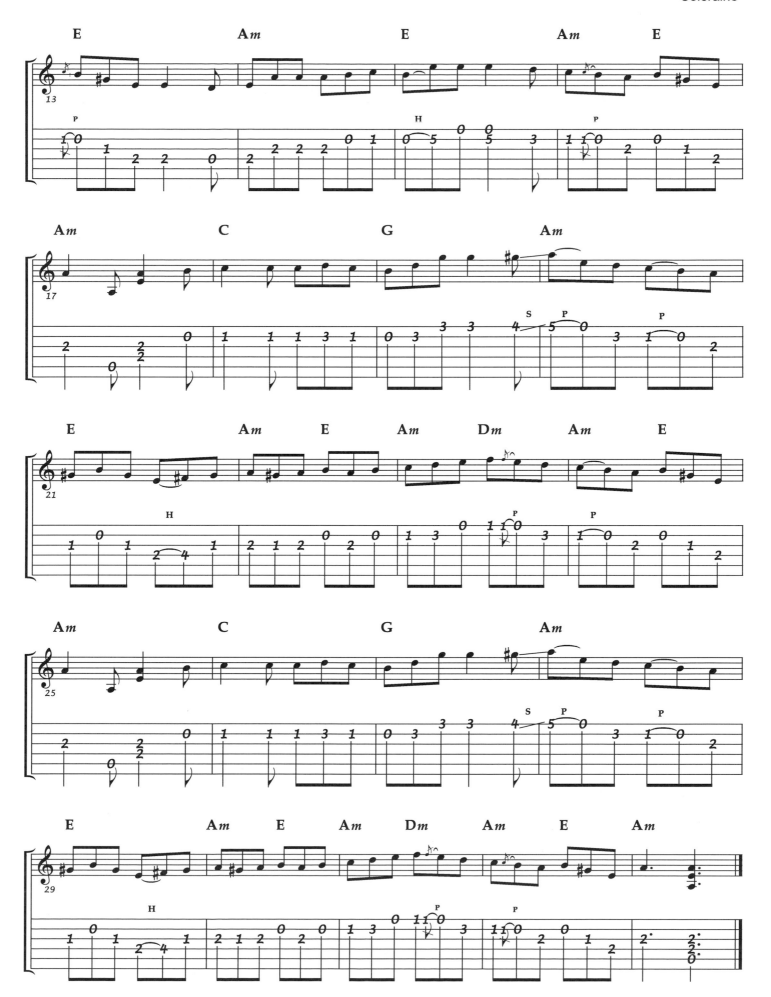

Photo by *Stefano Goldberg*

Scales

Scales are the backbone of musical knowledge and are a map of the proper notes to play when improvising, composing and performing melodies. Most people study the structure of scales for years. They memorize scales and develop their mechanisms. The luckier ones are able to listen, practice and find their way instinctively without too much theoretical study. This topic is the most widely studied and mastered by guitar methods, magazines, instructional videos and teachers of all styles, and every good—or would-be—guitarist either possesses or can easily find a large amount of study material on this subject.

On the other hand, material regarding the analysis of scales and arpeggios—and their use in the aesthetics of traditional music—is rare. This is exactly the aspect I would like to consider, and point out a series of specific approaches (often wrongfully overlooked) that guitarists who love acoustic sounds should combine with the study of the "cultured" schools.

This being said, I will move on to the practical aspects without lingering over topics that may be expanded elsewhere. I assume that the readers of this book already possess some material on the subject. What I recommend, however, is to achieve a basic knowledge that should include at least major and minor scales and arpeggios as well as major and minor pentatonic scales with the most important fingerings. Guitarists should also be familiar with the fundamental principles of how the different modes, with their distinctive sonorities and peculiarities, originate from a diatonic scale.

Open String Major Scales and Relative Minors

The first scale patterns to be covered in the aesthetics of root music are the open string scales. The easiest ones are those in the keys of C, D, E, F, G, A, B, of which, for completeness and clarity, it is recommended to learn the relative minors as well.

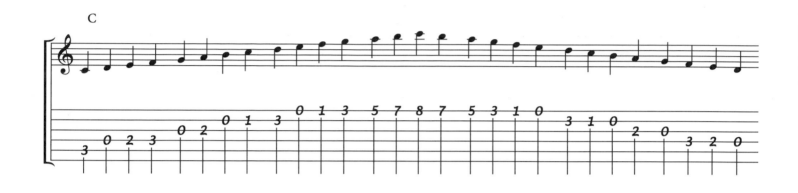

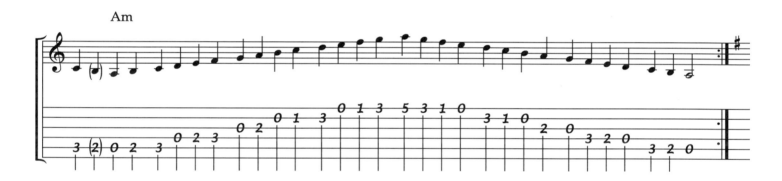

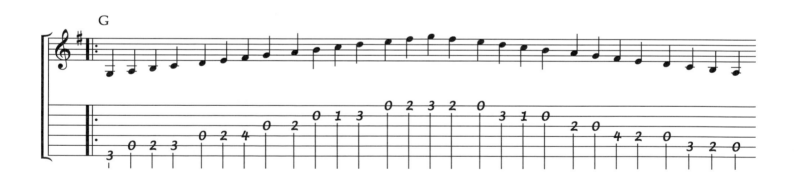

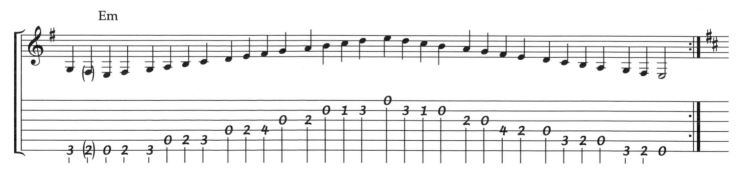

© 2010 Giuseppe Gambetta (SIAE - ITALIA)

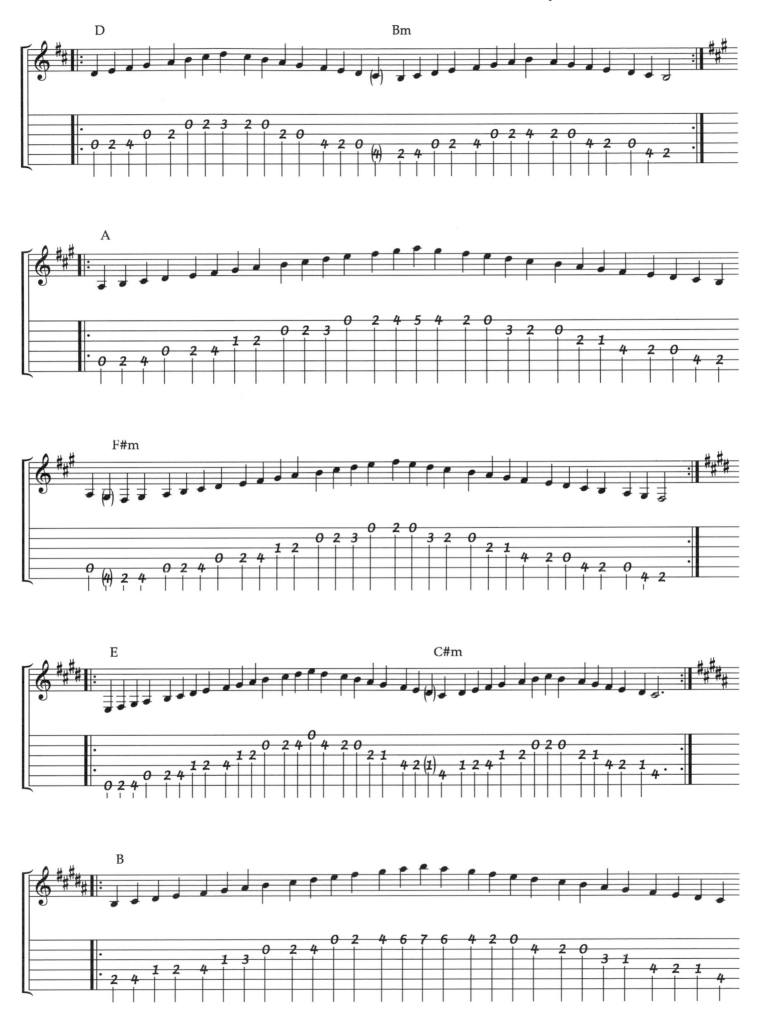

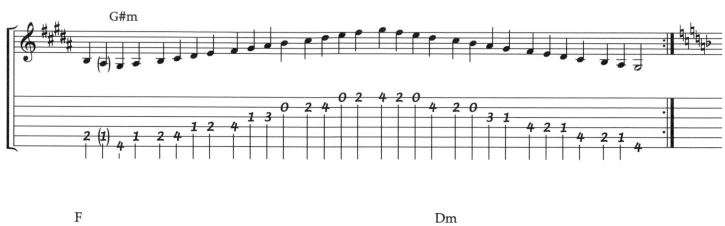

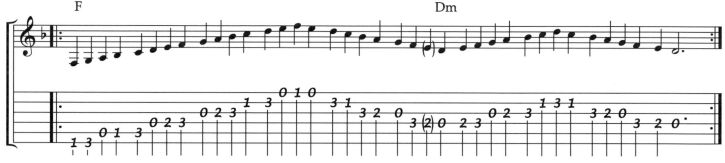

Open String Scales with Changes in Position

Another typical and highly distinctive sound is that of the scale patterns that make use of open strings when switching from one position to another (this is often the case with changes on the first, second and third string). The transition to the new position occurs while the open string is being played. Such technique makes the movement more fluent; at the same time, the sound is enriched by the overlapping of vibrating strings. This can in fact only be accomplished in certain keys, as shown in the following examples.

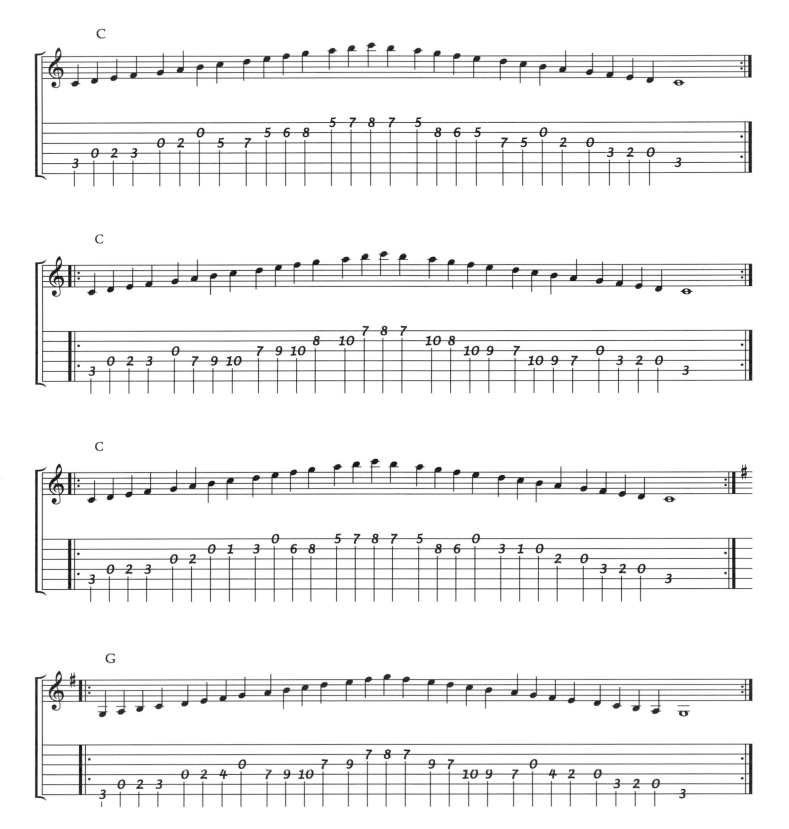

© 2010 Giuseppe Gambetta (SIAE - ITALIA)

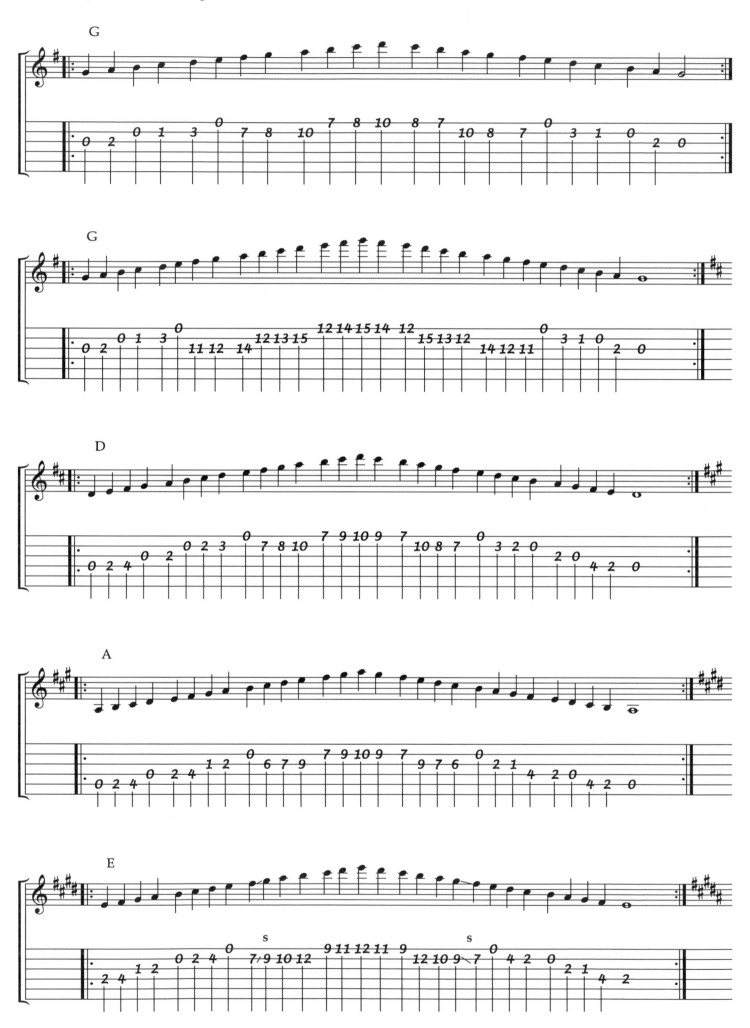

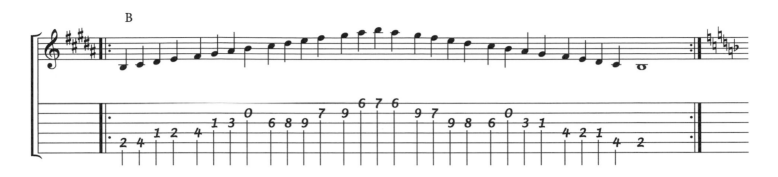

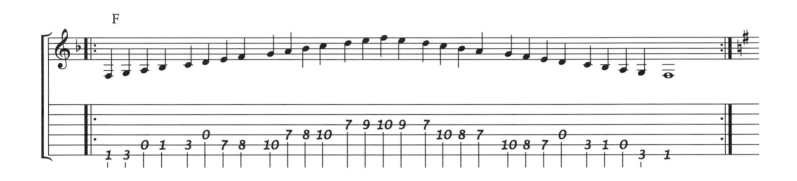

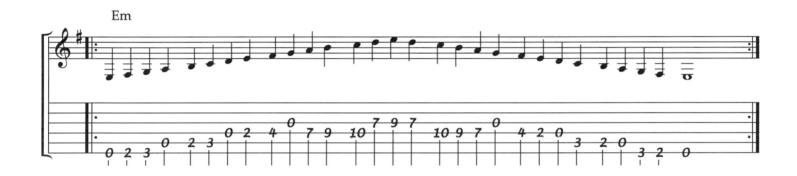

Scales with "Double Stops" on Open Strings

Scales that utilize double stops (notes played simultaneously on different strings sounding, in this case, in unison) are of great interest as they are an expression of the unique possibilities of stringed instruments. These sounds are often the heart of certain kinds of roots music. In the following example I will underline the possibility of accentuating certain notes of the scale with a double stop on two adjacent strings. Although this is an embellishment rather than a proper scale pattern, it is a sonority that should be incorporated in your study from the start, because it is the most common means to enrich phrasing in popular music.

Example: G Major Scale

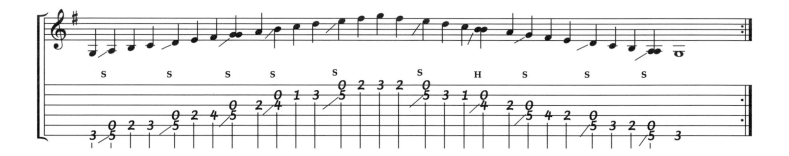

© 2010 Giuseppe Gambetta (SIAE - ITALIA)

Scales in Harp Style

The extreme example of scales with overlapping sounds is called Harp Style or Floating. In this case each note is always (or almost always) played on different strings. This technique is often used to build unique licks or melodic variations from the open sound. It is very difficult to build whole scales using this style, but it is sometimes possible to do so by an extended stretching of the left hand as in the following examples.

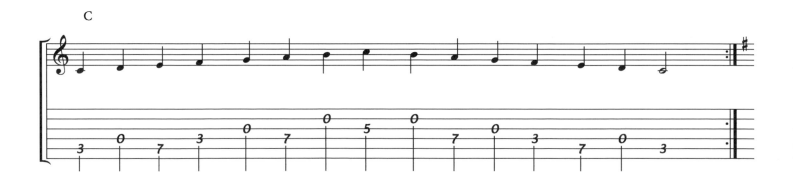

© 2010 Giuseppe Gambetta (SIAE - ITALIA)

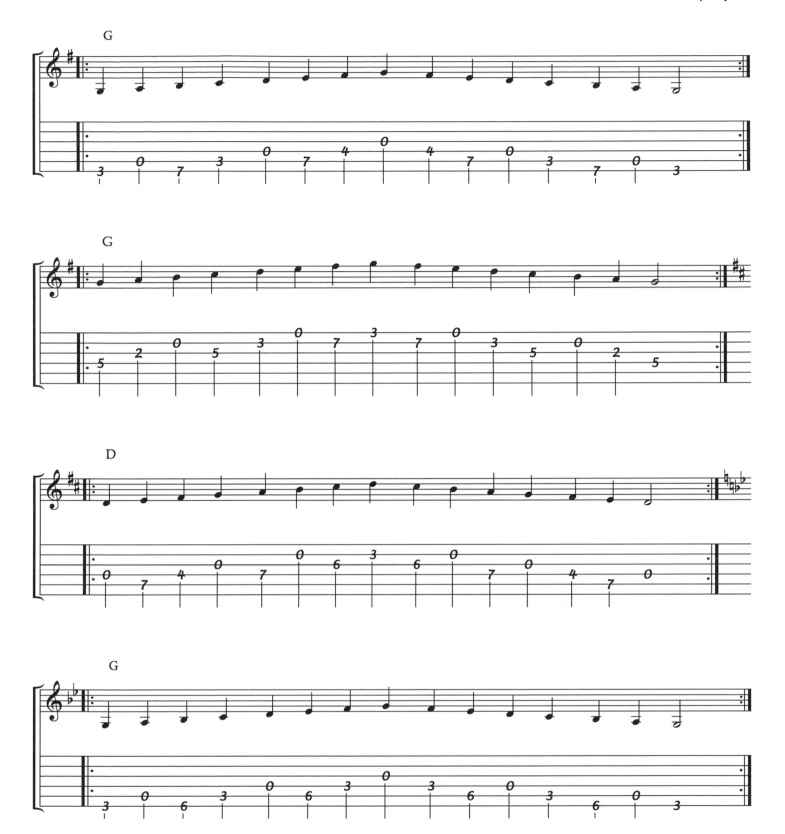

Scales with Drones

I would like to conclude with an example of a very important sound in roots music: the notes of the scale can be played with a drone as in the following exercise.

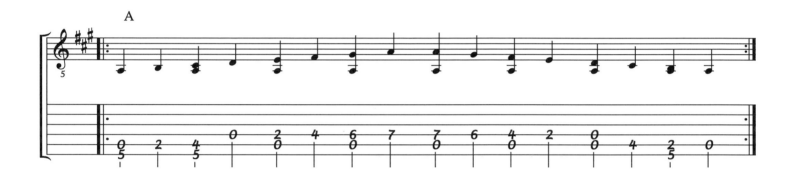

© 2010 Giuseppe Gambetta (SIAE - ITALIA)

Improvisation in roots music

In traditional music we will come across forms of improvisation developed over time in each region and culture. They display an aesthetic sense linked to the history, musicians and instruments. They may have dissimilar rules, of which the origins are often uncertain. I have always been fascinated by the exploration of this area so rich in ramifications. I try to improvise, listen to and study the great artists who have codified the sounds. I love going out to meet the performers of the tradition personally.

Harmonically speaking, these improvisations are often simpler than those heard in jazz music or in other cultured music genres, but they show structures and techniques of great complexity from other points of view.

The improvisations often draw inspiration from the driving rhythms of folk dances. The embellishments develop from the "traditional" usage of strings, which create special textures when ringing open. A fundamental characteristic of improvisation in roots music, compared to other forms, is the importance and the strong presence of the melodic line.
The relations with the melody are particularly tight, the presence and the return to the melodic line more consistent. When practicing improvisation, it is common to come across the variation or the embellishment right on the melody line.
In order to organize a study targeting a full comprehension and thorough analysis of these issues, I have subdivided the chapter according to these basic concepts: improvisation on the melody; improvisation on harmony; and the union of these two forms.

Recommended Videos and Bibliography:
David Grier, *Building Powerful Solos*, Homespun Tapes (DVD + TAB)
Brad Davis, *Flatpick Jam (vol. 1-4)*, Flatpicking Mercantile (DVD)
Russ Barenberg, *Exploring the Fingerboard*,
Homespun Tapes (TAB + 6 CD)
John Jorgenson, *Intermediate Gypsy Jazz Guitar*,
Flatpicking Guitar Magazine, 2005

Recommended Recordings:
Quintet Du Hot Club The France: Django Reinhardt & Stephan Grappelli
The Tony Rice Unit, *Mar West*, Rounder, 1980
Mark O'Connor, *Markology*, Rounder, 1977
David Grier, *I've Got the House to Myself*, Dreadnought, 2002
Julian Lage, *Sounding Point*, Emarcy 2009

11

MELODIC IMPROVISATION

Melodic improvisation implies performing the melody while filtering it through one's own musical taste and modifying it, but only to a point where the original melody is still recognizable. The listener must constantly feel the connection with the original melody, though modified and integrated in many different ways, with embellishments, in the notes, rhythm, tone, etc. Each tradition has specific mechanisms and aesthetic rules that determine how far you can deviate from the original melody.

Among the different schools, the Celtic one seems to be the most respectful to the melody—which is never modified—and here the great performers distinguish themselves by their particular taste for ornamentation and musical expression. In other traditions, the variation on the original melodic line is more commonly accepted and some believe that the best improvisation upon a melody is the creation of a new melodic line that recalls the original melody as a whole, but acquires its own identity and autonomy. Some artists even state that the best way of improvising on the melody is playing the song as if you were composing it simultaneously.

To improvise "recomposing" the melody to one's own taste is a process that involves the most profound and complicated aspects of the artist's creativity. Those who decide to work in this direction can also develop very simple but effective concepts, such as filling the pauses in the melodic line, creating spaces by skipping notes of secondary importance, or playing notes with different durations, anticipating or delaying them. Something more difficult, but appropriate to the guitar, is to improvise second guitar voices and use drone notes. Of course, the best exercise is to set a task: locate the notes of a melodic line and start working on it, interpreting and embellishing it in every possible way.

Here's an example of this sort of exercise on "Scarborough Fair", a traditional tune known worldwide. I first transcribed the simple melody, then the melody with the embellishments only and finally the modified tune.

Scarborough Fair

Traditional,
arranged by Beppe Gambetta

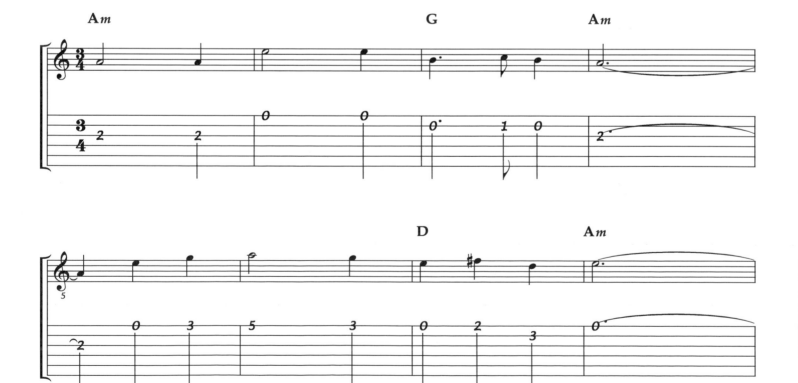

© 2010 Giuseppe Gambetta (SIAE - ITALIA)

Scarborough Fair

HARMONY IMPROVISATION

Harmony improvisation has no relationship with the melody of the song, but is solely based on phrases and variations connected with the chord progression.

The first important step in this direction is to memorize the chord progression so precisely as to always be aware of the underlying chords and harmonic progressions, even when engaged in improvising. Also in traditional music, harmony improvisation is based on the use and knowledge of scales and arpeggios, but apart from this common base, improvisation is built upon a fundamental mechanism based on the use of the so-called licks (stock patterns or phrases, already assimilated and prepared), which can be inserted according to personal taste and adjusted to the tune in the development of guitar phrasing. Guitar licks are a peculiar topic that deserves to be discussed in a separate chapter. Please refer to chapter 12 for an in-depth study regarding this subject. Those who want to examine the inner workings of harmony improvisation in depth will surely find help and information following the cultured schools and referring to a good jazz guitar method.

In folk music, various methods to simplify the mechanisms exist, such as locating the "right" notes, thinking about the positions of the chords on the fretboard or creating a visual map of the main points in which the phrasing must fall. Across the twelve frets of the octave the positions of each chord can be found three times. They can be interpreted as complete (on all six strings) or built on a limited number of strings. There are many phrases that have most of the "key" notes in these positions. This relationship is so obvious that you can tie phrasing and position together, as if the one was a direct expression of the other. The following examples start right from the three main positions of the major chords for the development of a phrase. The exercise consists of fluently transposing the phrasing to the different keys.

Improvising on Chord Positions

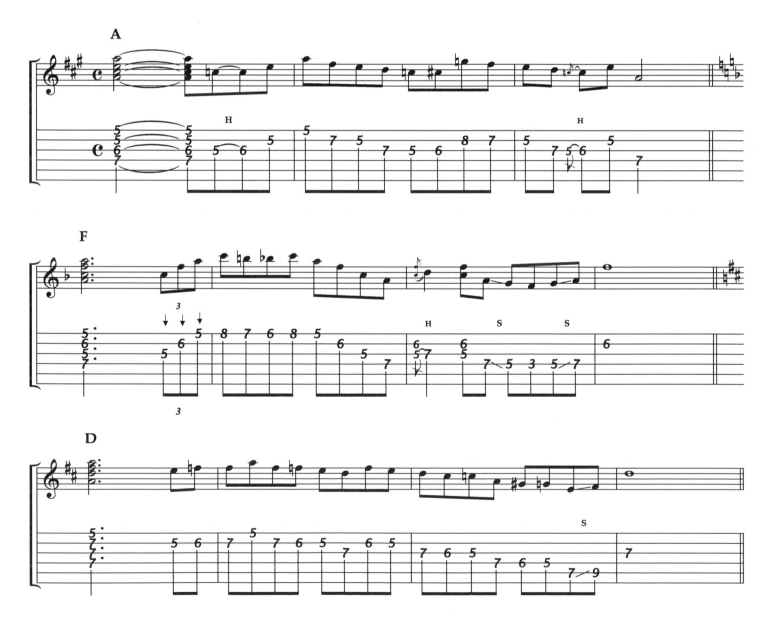

COMBINE AND ALTERNATE THE TWO FORMS

Experience in playing roots music helps to develop an aesthetic sense for alternating and merging these two kinds of improvisation in different ways.

The most immediate method is to alternate melodic solo sections and harmony solo sections. The first are more present in the initial phase and the second mostly at the end, in a dynamic crescendo where the phrasing is generally freer from the melody and takes over at the end of the song.

"The House of the Rising Sun" shows the four steps into which you can divide the exercise in order to work on these different characteristics that you should practice: first, the precise melodic line; second, the variations on the melody; third, variations on the chord progression; and, finally, the mixed variations.

The House of the Rising Sun

Traditional,
arranged by Beppe Gambetta

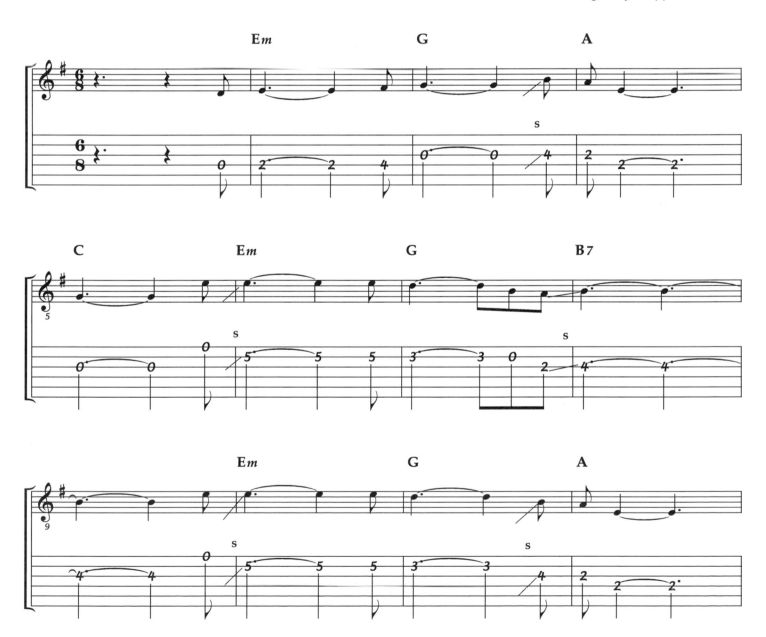

© 2010 Giuseppe Gambetta (SIAE - ITALIA)

The House of the Rising Sun

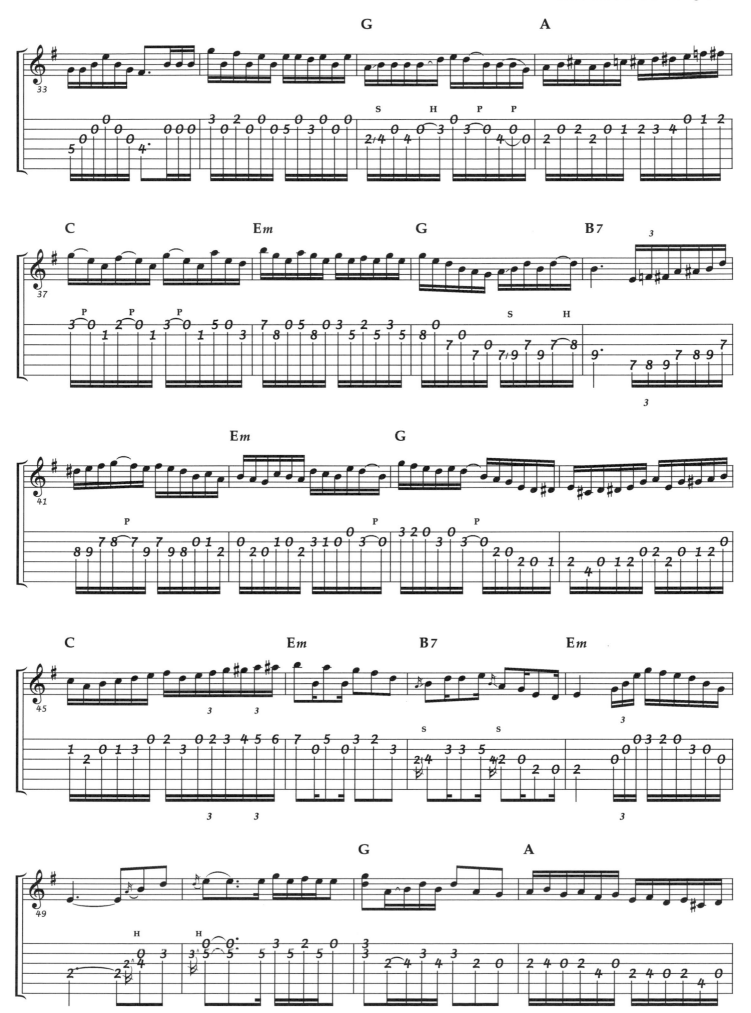

The House of the Rising Sun

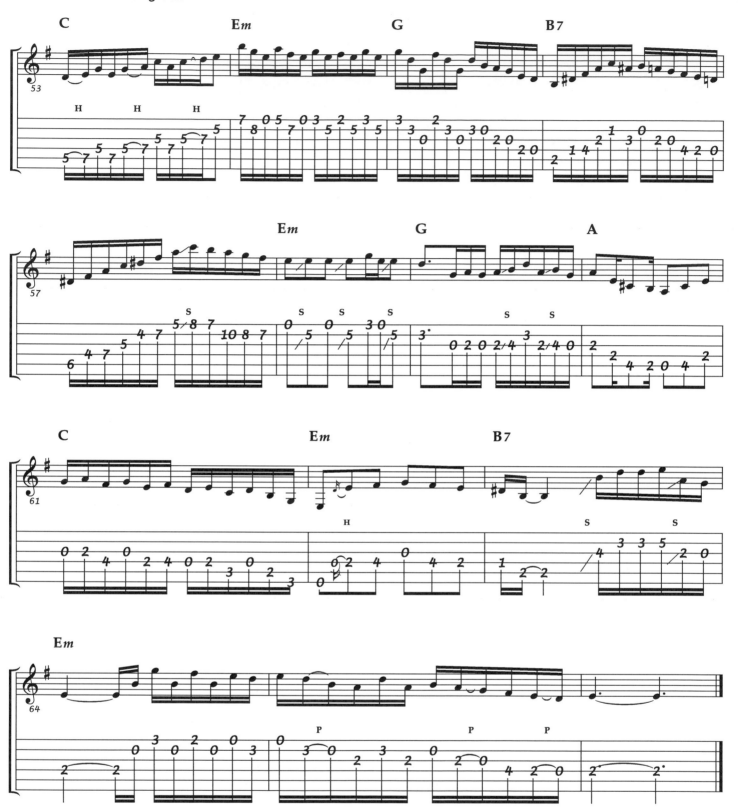

Among my arrangements, "The Battle of Waterloo" (from the CD "Rendez-vous"—Gadfly Records, 2008), is a good example of solo in which the original melody appears in different stages. This is a detailed transcription.

Battle of Waterloo

Guitar Solo

Capo on the 2nd fret

Traditional,
arranged by Beppe Gambetta

© 2010 Giuseppe Gambetta (SIAE - ITALIA)

Battle of Waterloo

Photo by *Alessandro Zunino*

Licks

Licks are musical phrases and creative fragments characteristic of a particular style. They are often selected from those created by the most important artists of the genre and revised to be used as basic elements for improvisation.

They are the fastest way to directly enter the aesthetics and dynamics of a chosen genre; a dip into a pre-packaged palette of selected notes.
Working with licks means developing sensitivity together with the ability to insert the right phrases in the most suitable places during improvisation. There is the risk, however, of remaining trapped within the pre-packaged licks, resulting in an impersonal, sterile approach to improvisation.

The creation of licks in a personal style (not copied from others), is a great sign of maturity and artistic personality. The hardest part is not learning the phrase, but understanding how to use it during improvisation. Phrases should be performed instinctively, ideally connected with the key of the tune and the right moment to enter them has to be chosen with great care.

Licks can be memorized by the keys, but also on the basis of the artist who created them, of the style they refer to, and of the technical features.

Recommended Videos and Bibliography:
Brad Davis, *Improvising Bluegrass Guitar*,
Musician's Workshop, 1998 (CD + TAB)
Bryan Sutton, *Secrets for Successfull Flatpicking*,
Homespun Tapes (DVD + TAB)
Joe Carr, *60 Hot Licks for Bluegrass Guitar*,
Texas Music Video (DVD + TAB)

Recommended Recordings:
Bryan Sutton, *Ready to Go*, Sugar Hill, 2005
Jim Hurst, *A Box of Chocolates*, 2007
Chet Atkins, *Mark Knopfler*, Neck & Neck, Sony, 1990

Licks in the Style of the Masters

The following examples are licks inspired by Doc Watson, Tony Rice, Clarence White, the masters of the style. The last two examples concern cross-pollination—licks that are common to artists of distant musical genres.

© 2010 Giuseppe Gambetta (SIAE - ITALIA)

Clarence White

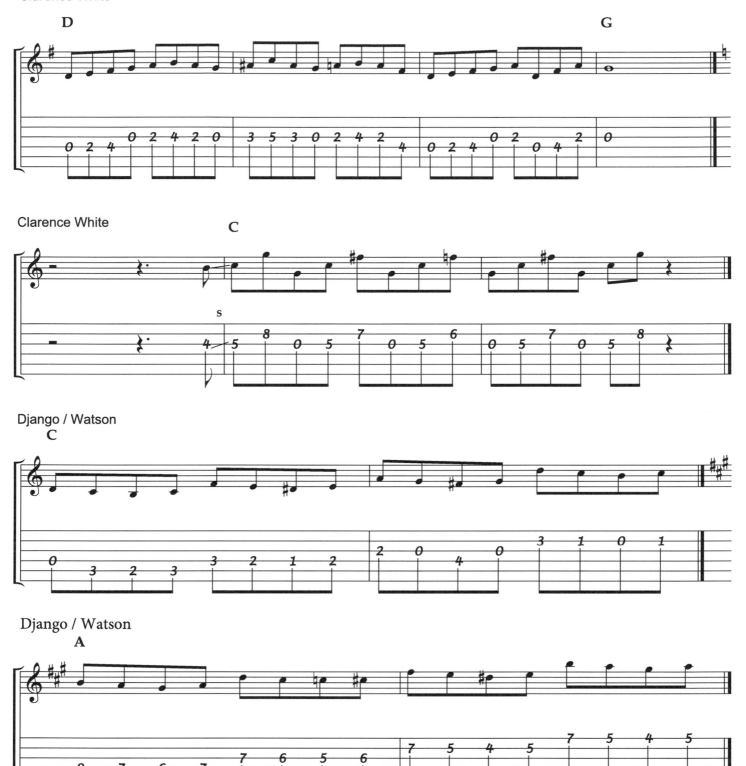

Clarence White

Django / Watson

Django / Watson

Licks Based on Particular Techniques

The next few licks are listed according to the particular technique they are played with: double-stop licks are played on two different strings with a second simultaneous note; harp-style licks are played with a choice of notes that always fall on different strings, and the overlapping sounds create a harp effect; slide licks are based on a predominant use of glissando; and *down-down-up* licks are based on the *down-down-up* movement of the pick on two adjacent strings, an interesting development of crosspicking.

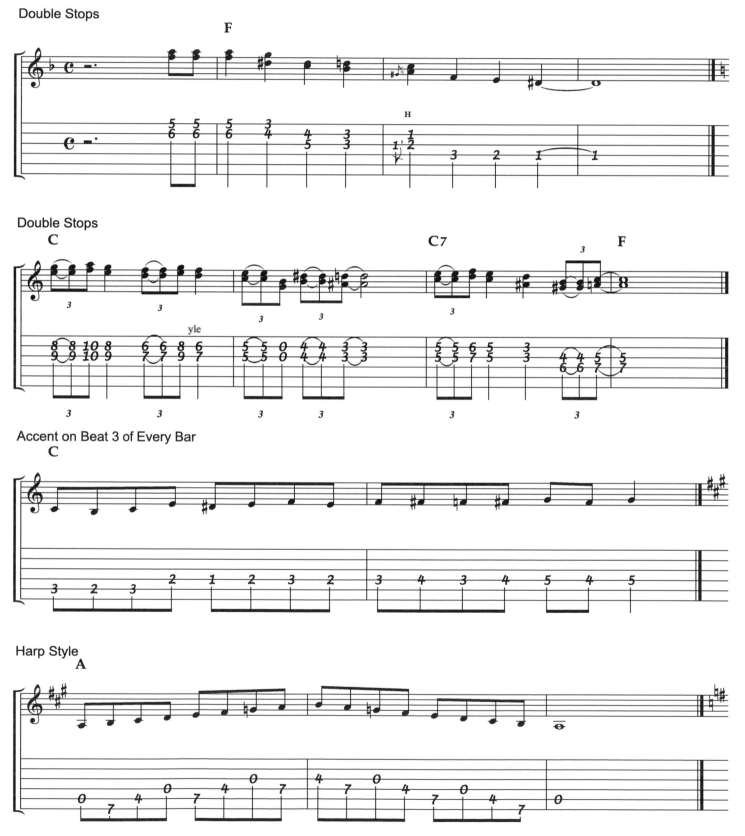

© 2010 Giuseppe Gambetta (SIAE - ITALIA)

Harp Style

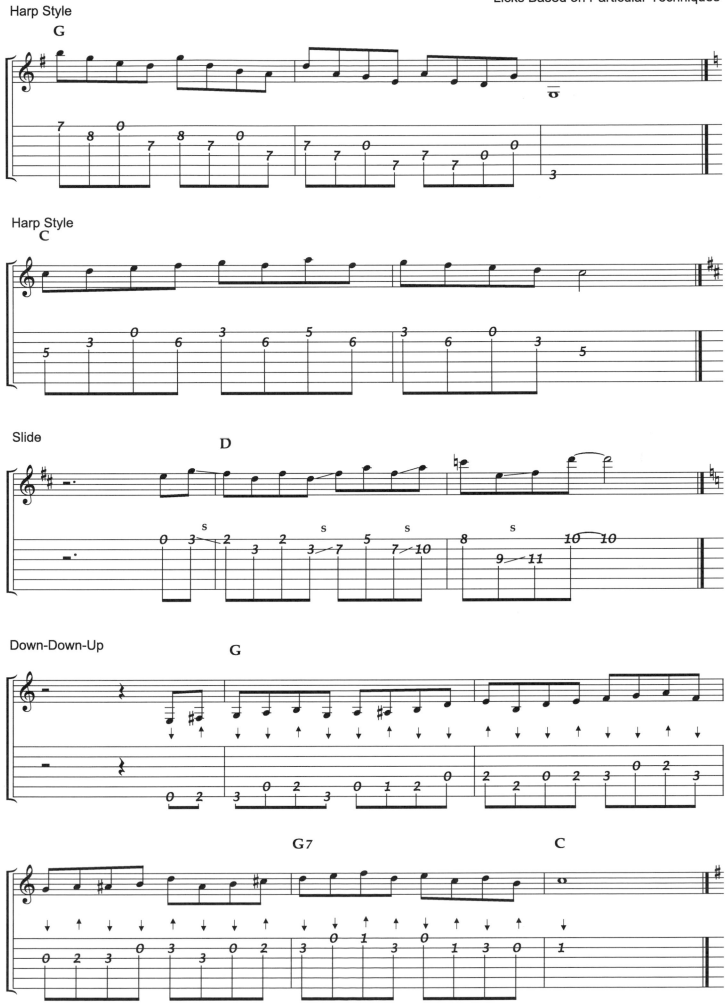

Down-Down-Up

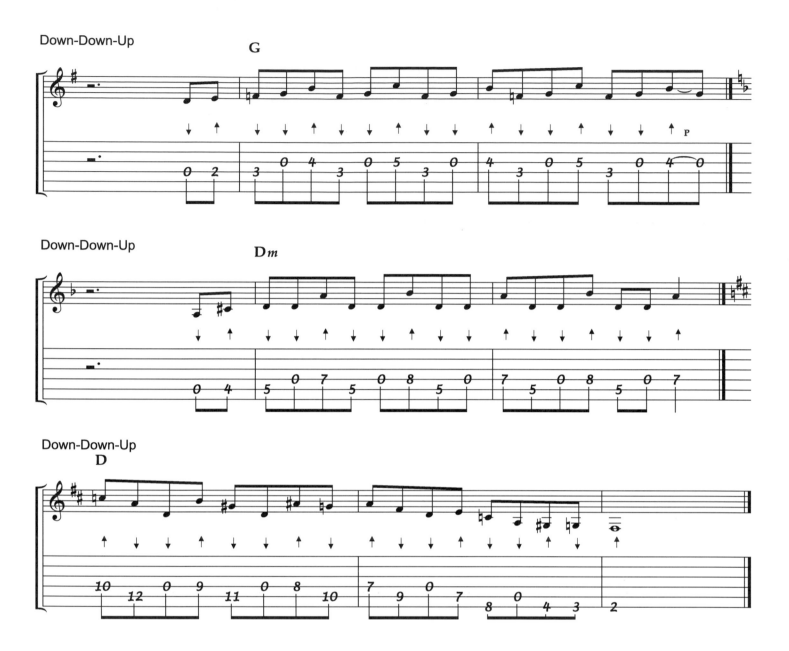

Licks in the Style of...

Finally, the last set of licks refers to specific sounds of diverse styles of acoustic music.

© 2010 Giuseppe Gambetta (SIAE - ITALIA)

Licks in the style of...

Nashville Country

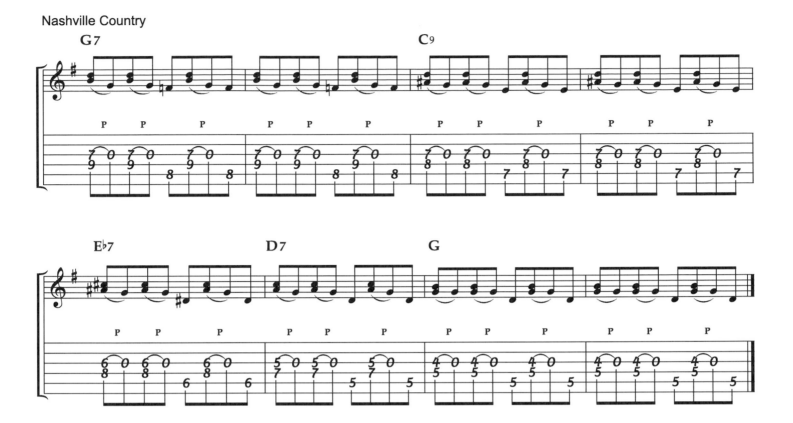

The best approach for those who want to start playing with licks is substitution. The idea behind this approach is to learn how to replace small parts of an already known phrase with new licks. This should be done gradually: even throwing a single lick into a basic melody can initially be considered an important step towards the usage and proper adjustment of these small phrases within your music.

Another fundamental exercise, and one of the most difficult parts of effective improvisation, is in exiting the lick. In most cases, those who improvise do nothing but assemble phrases and notes from scales they already know how to play. Still, the best ideas often arise when known phrases are applied to different contexts.

Technically, it is not very difficult to play licks you already know, when your fingers move almost automatically. Things get harder when it is time to connect one phrase to another, namely when a new idea needs to be applied quickly, perhaps simultaneously with a chord change. A simple but effective procedure to get out of a tricky situation is to analyse the harmonic function of the lick. You can experiment on how to exit a lick by adjusting its final part to the new chord transition or to other new licks.

One of my compositions that is useful for learning the transition between licks is "Slade Stomp" (from the CD of the same name, Gadfly Records, 2006). It is an ironic stomp, written to commemorate Charles "Slade" Sawtelle, a great flatpicker who died prematurely in 1997.

Slade Stomp

Beppe Gambetta

© 2006 Giuseppe Gambetta (SIAE - ITALIA)

Slade Stomp

121

Slade Stomp

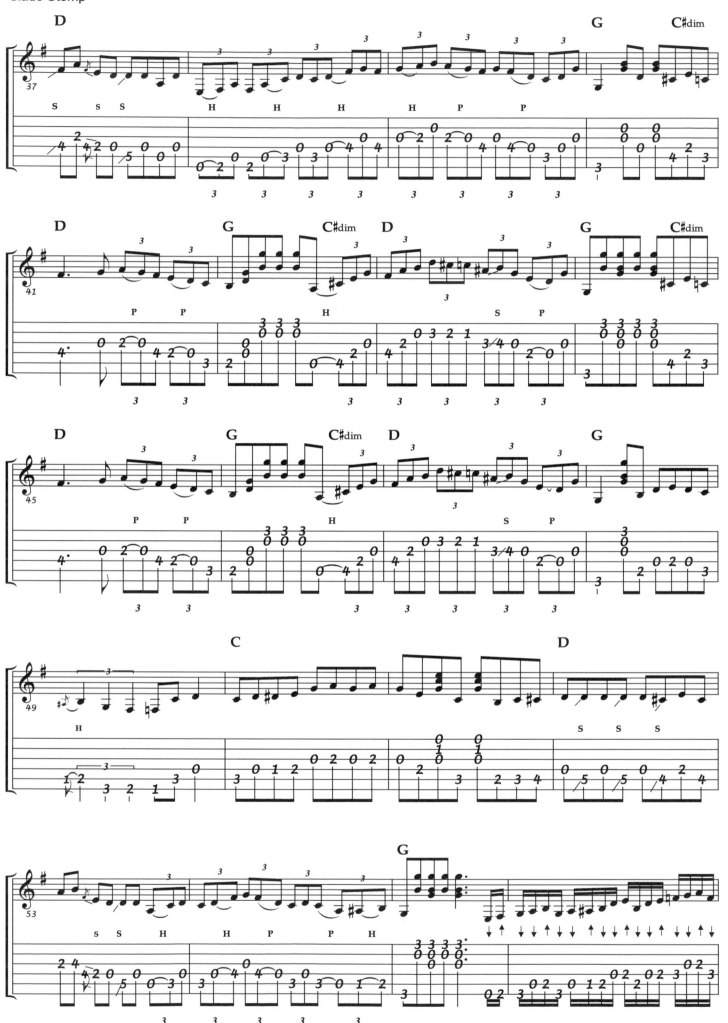

Photo by *Stefano Goldberg*

Open Tunings

Open tunings have not been used very much by American flatpickers, probably because they were considered unsuitable for the traditional sound, and too "risky" to be applied in the context of a band.

To find examples of free and creative picking in open tuning, one has to look among the repertoires of creative geniuses of diverse and progressive styles. The late Michael Hedges produced interesting examples of flatpicked guitar in open tuning.

Flatpickers of the British Isles are much more innovative in this field, as their approach to folk revival has often been open to experimentation. In the '70s Davey Graham pioneered the DADGAD tuning, widely used in the traditional context but also adopted as the main tuning by great contemporary acoustic artists. Alternate tunings give the instrument a new soul and allow one to engage in new forms of musical expression.

While exploring new tunings, one experiences the pleasure of discovering sounds impossible to achieve with standard tunings and, at the same time, the loss of the concepts related to the knowledge of the fretboard. When using any kind of open tuning, a fundamental step is to learn the new fingerings for the scales and chords. As an example and starting point, here are the fingerings for the most common scales in DADGAD and DGDGAD tunings.

Recommended Videos and Bibliography:
Mark Hanson, *Alternate Tunings*, Accent on Music
Beppe Gambetta, *Originals*, Carisch, 2010
Beppe Gambetta, *Blu di Genova* (Guitar Transcriptions), Mel Bay, 2010
Various Artists, *Alternate Tunings Guitar Essentials*, String Letter Publishing, 2000
Beppe Gambetta, *New Directions in Flatpicking*, Homespun Tapes (DVD + TAB)

Recommended Recordings:
Michael Hedges, *Oracle*, Whindham Hill 1996
Beppe Gambetta, *Rendez-vous*, Gadfly Records, 2008
Tony McManus, *Tony McManus*, Greentrax Recordings 1995

Essential Scales in DADGAD Tuning

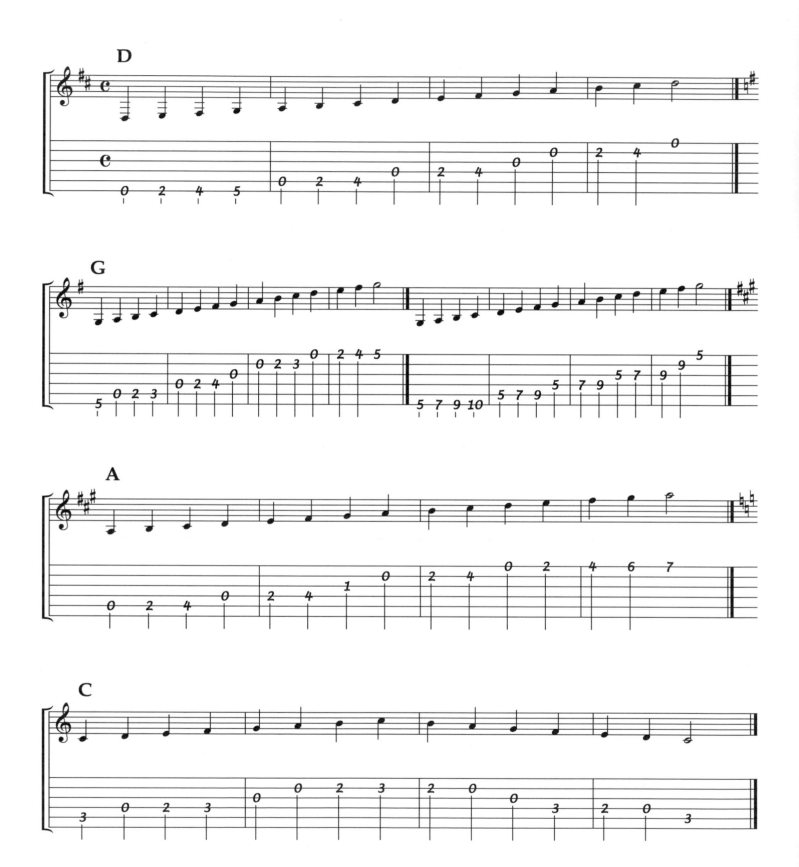

Essential Scales in DGDGAD Tuning

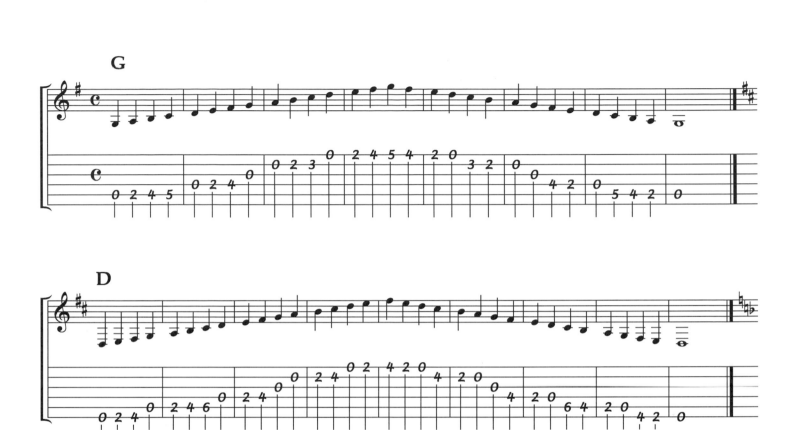

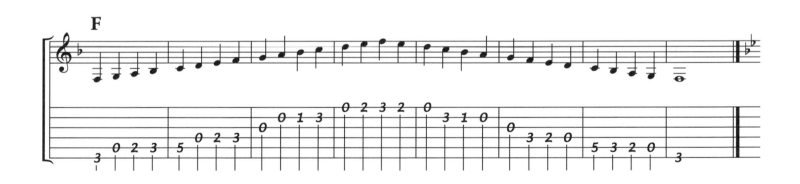

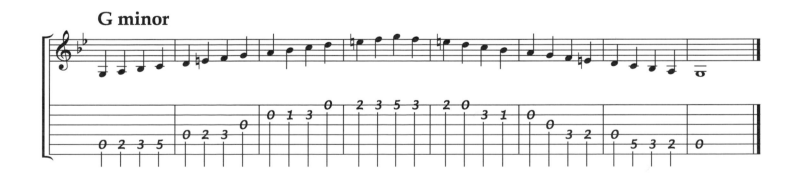

"Aires de Pontevedra" is a traditional tune of Galicia, a region in northwest Spain with a strong Celtic heritage that can be heard in the notes of this song. DADGAD tuning seems born to fit this melody, which often resounds naturally on adjacent strings without requiring numerous changes or difficult transitions.

Aires de Pontevedra

Tuning: D A D G A D

Galician traditional melody,
arranged by Beppe Gambetta

© 2010 Giuseppe Gambetta (SIAE - ITALIA)

Aires de Pontevedra

My composition "Procession" (from the "Rendez-vous" CD), on the other hand, uses DGDGAD tuning. This is a variation of the previous tuning that allows you to easily play both in the key of G and in the key of D, if necessary. The song is an aggregate of different uses of "ethnic" crosspicking and the use of drone strings on guitar.

Procession

Tuning: D G D G A D

Capo on the 2nd fret

Beppe Gambetta

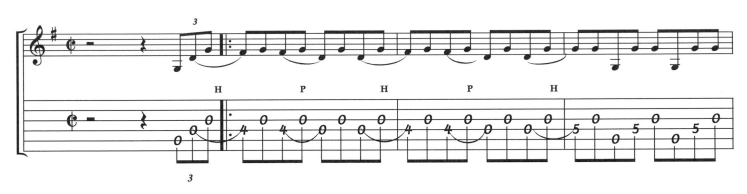

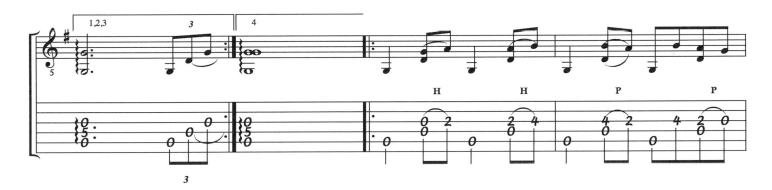

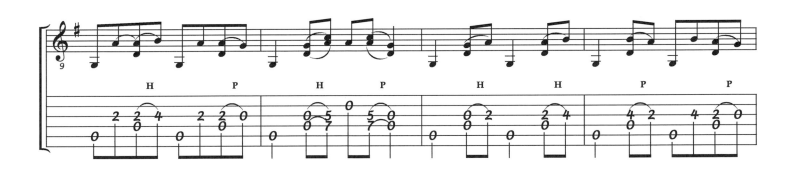

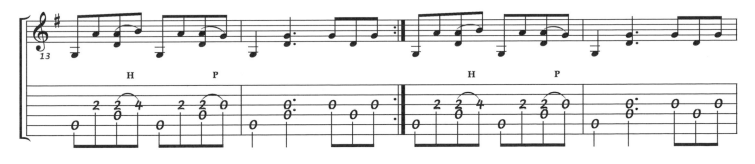

© 2008 Giuseppe Gambetta (SIAE - ITALIA)

Procession

Sestrina is a melody that comes from the repertoire of the *piferro*, an ancient Italian traditional reed instrument of the Apennines. I chose DADEAE tuning after experimenting for a long time with other open tunings in search of one that could fully express the charm of the tune. The arrangement comes from the "Blu Di Genova" CD and has been added to the medley at the end of the song "A Cimma" by Fabrizio De Andrè.

Sestrina

Tuning: D A D E A E

Capo on the 2nd fret

Italian traditional dance,
arranged by Beppe Gambetta

© 2002 Giuseppe Gambetta (SIAE - ITALIA)

Sestrina

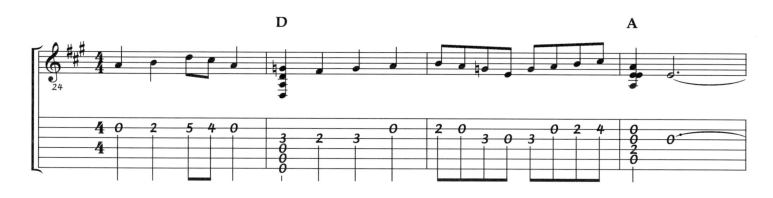

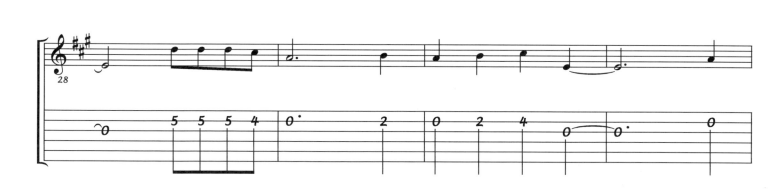

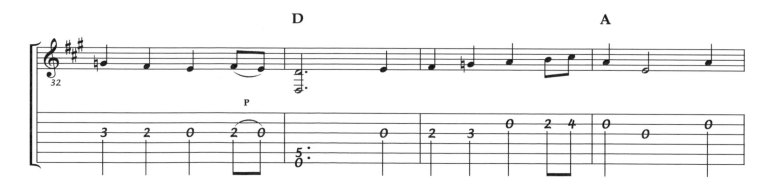

Ending

"Tarantexas" (another original composition from the "Blu Di Genova" CD) is a typical example of cross pollination
—a synthesis of elements from different cultures that meet and communicate in DADGAD tuning.

Tarantexas

Tuning: D A D G A D

Free Intro

Beppe Gambetta

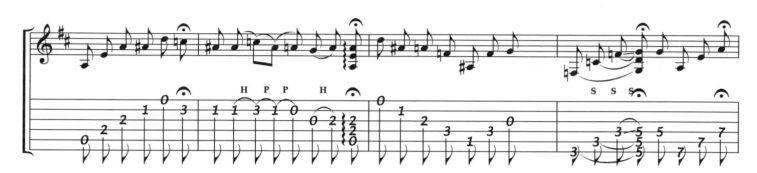

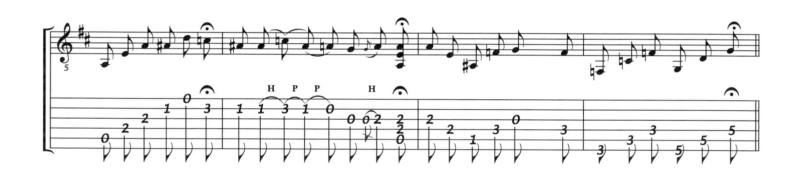

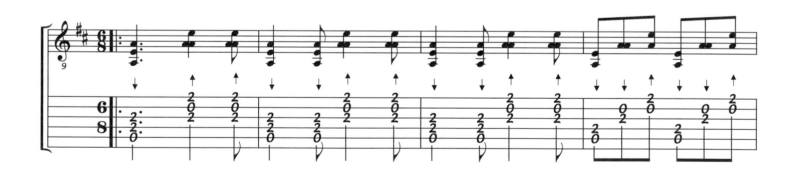

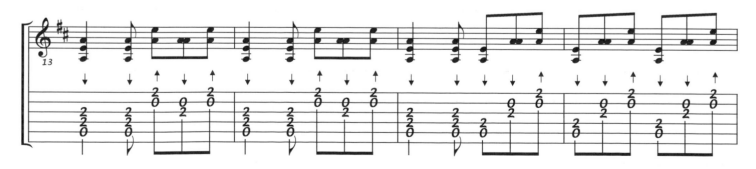

© 2002 Giuseppe Gambetta (SIAE - ITALIA)

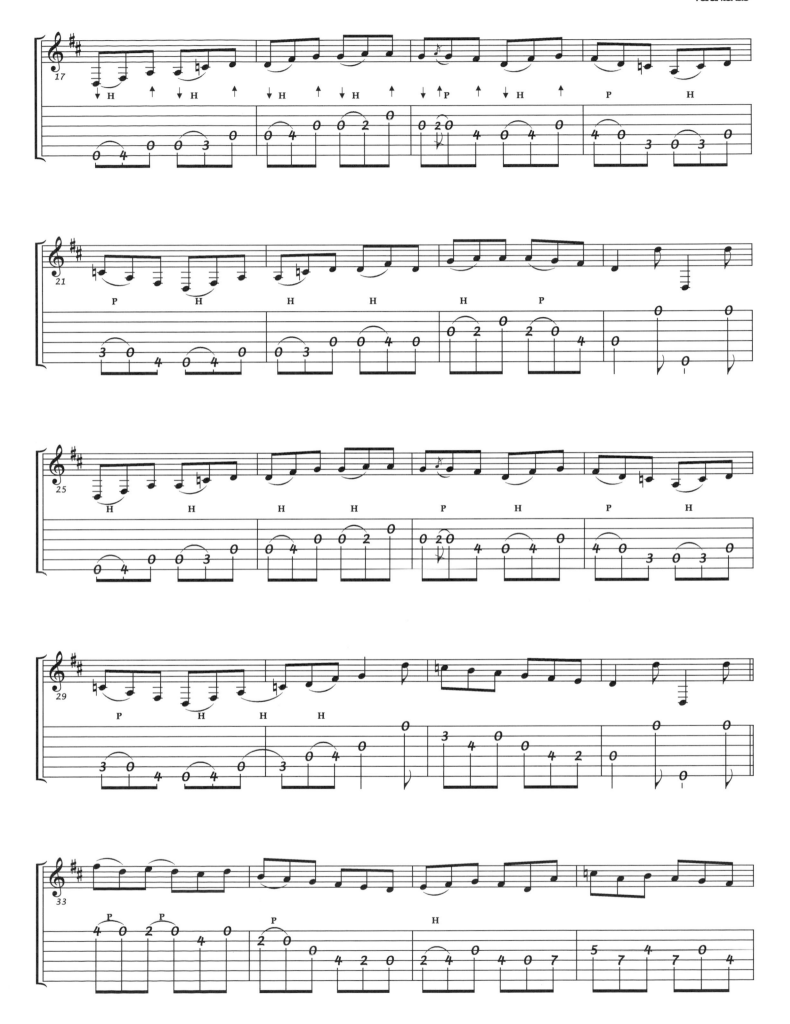

Tarantexas

Last time to Coda

Tarantexas

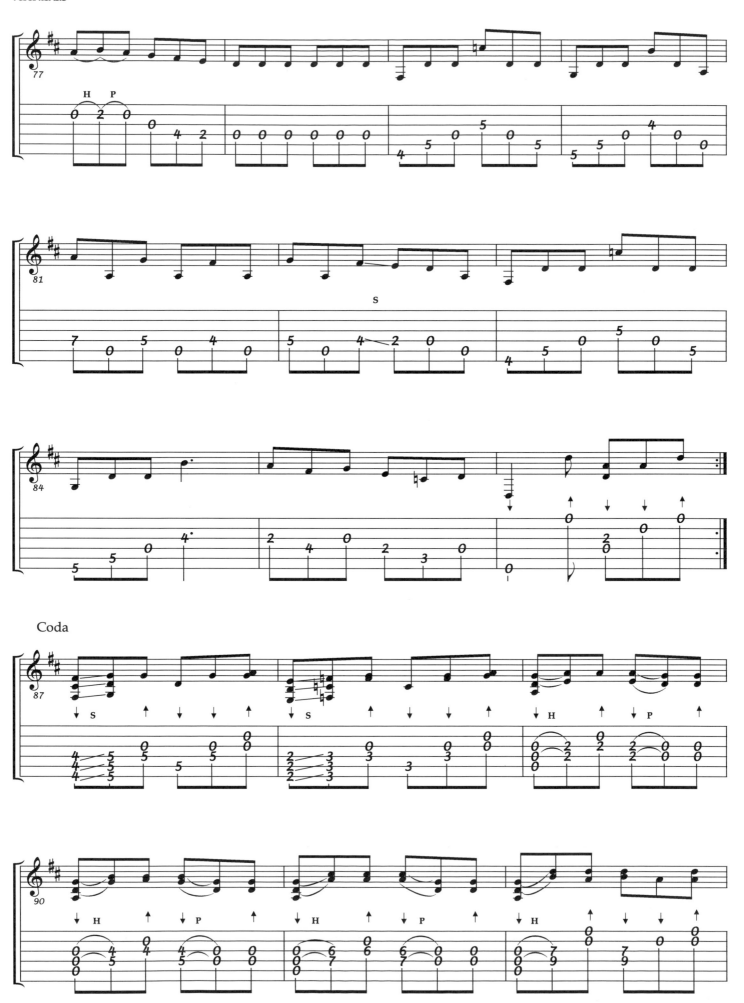

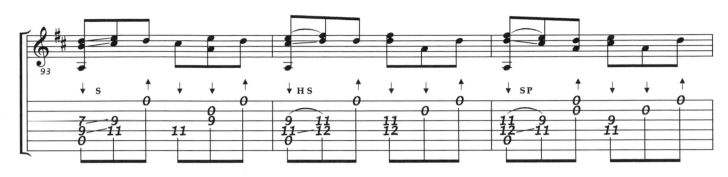

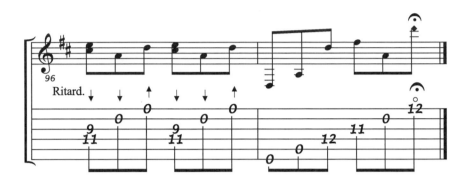

Photo by *Giorgio Scarfì*

The Solo Guitarist in Flatpicking Style

This is a unique art that I got into and have developed throughout my career. At first, the choice was dictated by the need to travel and to offer independent and essentially soloist concerts at an affordable cost, allowing me to move easily across any distance and transport my music around the world. From this practical need, my artistic evolution has brought me to new sounds, techniques and tricks to overcome the objective limit of using a pick that, by its nature, cannot pluck non-adjacent strings simultaneously, like the fingers of a hand can do with arpeggios. Building a flatpicking soloist repertoire is a big challenge. The examples of flatpicking solos from which one can gain inspiration are very rare because the great masters almost always played as a duo or with an ensemble.

The main technical problem is, clearly, to create a wide and complex sound texture despite having a pick as the only source. The challenge of creating arpeggios and playing notes on non-adjacent strings simultaneously is sometimes impossible to win, but when the solution is found it often has a peculiar character, sometimes a sound never heard before.

The technique of highlighting the final note of the melody when strumming a chord (seen in chapter 5) is certainly the most intuitive and commonly used method of expanding the sound texture, but there are many other possible tricks that can be used.

For example, a low note and a high note on non-adjacent strings can be played at short interval by slightly anticipating or delaying a note, and playing fast jumps on your pick, creating an *acciaccatura* that often produces a pleasant effect. A simultaneous sound can also be achieved by playing a pull-off or a hammer-on while you pick a note on a nonadjacent string. Sometimes, a sound impossible to achieve in standard tuning can be easily obtained in open tuning. It requires a lot of patience to explore the different options and find the suitable tuning, evaluating the different sonorities obtained. In order to play flatpicking guitar style exclusively, it is necessary to acquire specific technical skills, such as not stopping string vibration or, conversely, muting a string that should not be played.

For those who want to listen to some interesting examples of this style, here is a list of songs that accompanied my studies over the years: Doc Watson's solo performance of "Black Mountain Rag", "When You Are Smiling" by Clarence White, "The Old Brown Case" by Norman Blake, "Church Street Blues" by Tony Rice, Dan Crary Lady's Fancy.

Recommended Videos and Bibliography:
Tony Rice, *An Intimate Lesson with Tony Rice*, Homespun Tapes (DVD+TAB)

Recommended Recordings:
Doc Watson, *The Essential Doc Watson*, Vanguard, 1990
Clarence White, *Flatpick*, Sierra Records
Norman Blake, The Fields of November, Flying Fish, 1991
Tony Rice, *Church Street Blues*, Sugar Hill, 1993
Dan Crary, *Lady's Fancy*, Sugar Hill, 1977
Django Reinhardt, *In Solitaire*

The songs that I suggest are examples of totally different sonorities, but with the common peculiarity of being soloistic flatpicking.

"Deus Ti Salvet Maria" is a wonderful traditional Sardinian *Hail Mary* regarded by many as one of the island's anthems. The performance of this tune represents one of the most intense moments in my concerts, proving that melody and poetry can sometimes beat virtuosity and speed-picking. This is an example of a traditional tune transcribed for guitar. In order to accomplish the arrangement, I came up with a complex form of tremolo based on the *down-down-up* movement that helps sustain the notes of the vocal part.

Deus Ti Salvet Maria
(Sardinian Ave Maria)

Tuning: D G D G A D

Capo on the 3rd fret

Traditional,
arranged by Beppe Gambetta

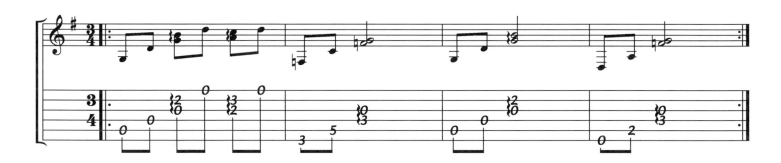

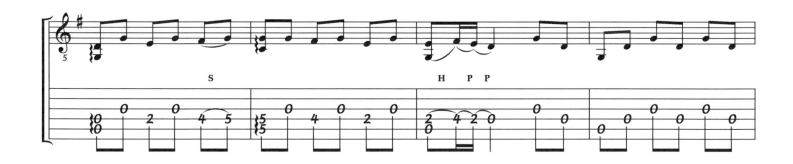

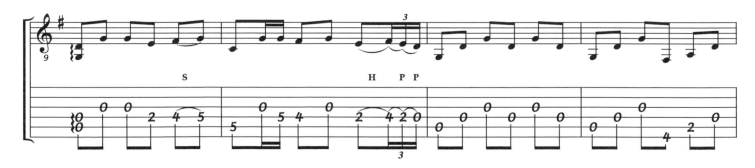

© 2006 Giuseppe Gambetta (SIAE - ITALIA)

Deus Ti Salvet Maria

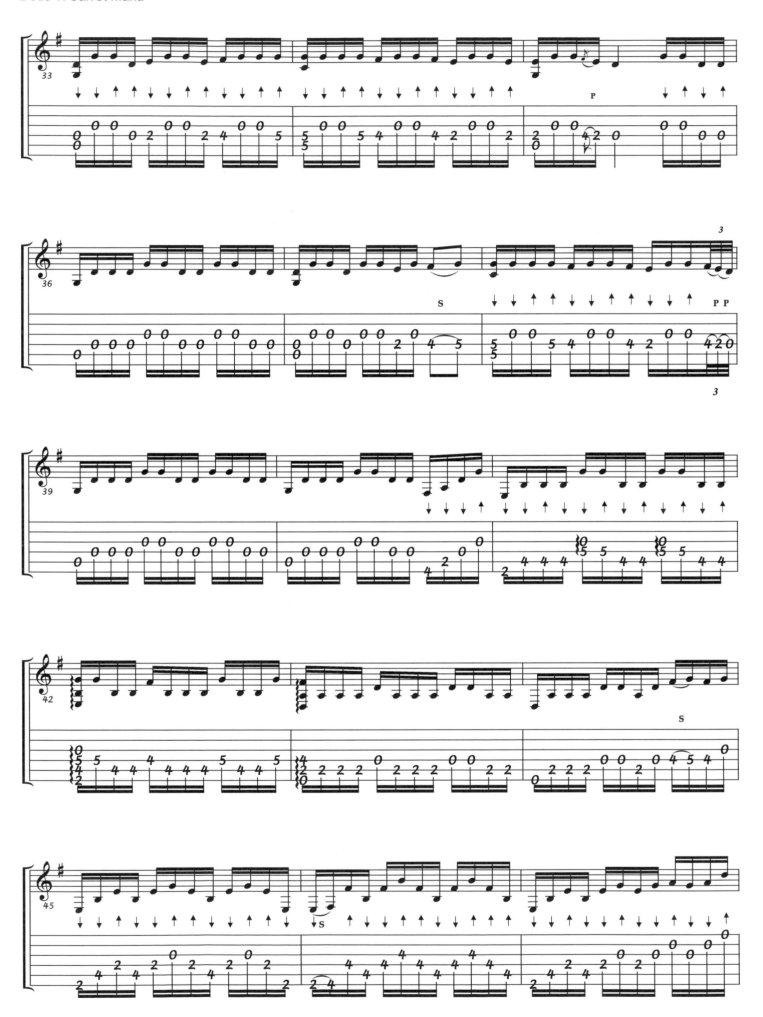

"On The Road With Mama" combines the rhythm of a southern Italian dance with a blues-rock sound, an example of cross pollination that joins the two shores of the ocean. A 3D animated cartoon that has been seen all over the world was created for this music (http://www.youtube.com/watch?v=R8k_DMHUxbA).

On the Road with Mama

Tuning: D A D G A D

Beppe Gambetta

© 2002 Giuseppe Gambetta (SIAE - ITALIA)

On The Road With Mama

On The Road With Mama

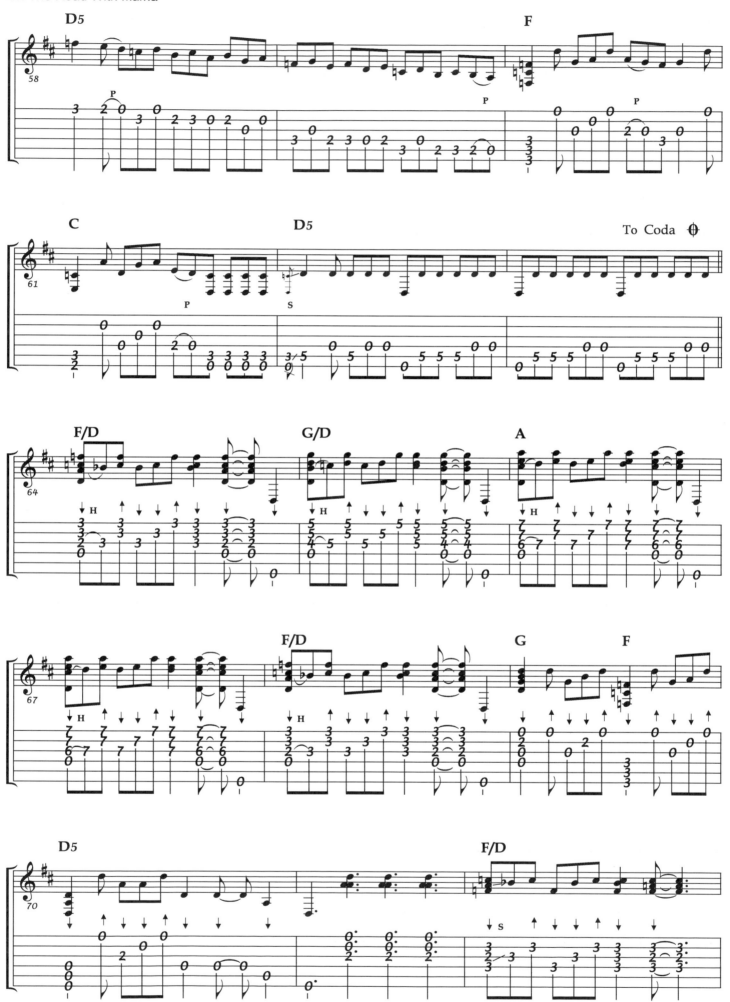

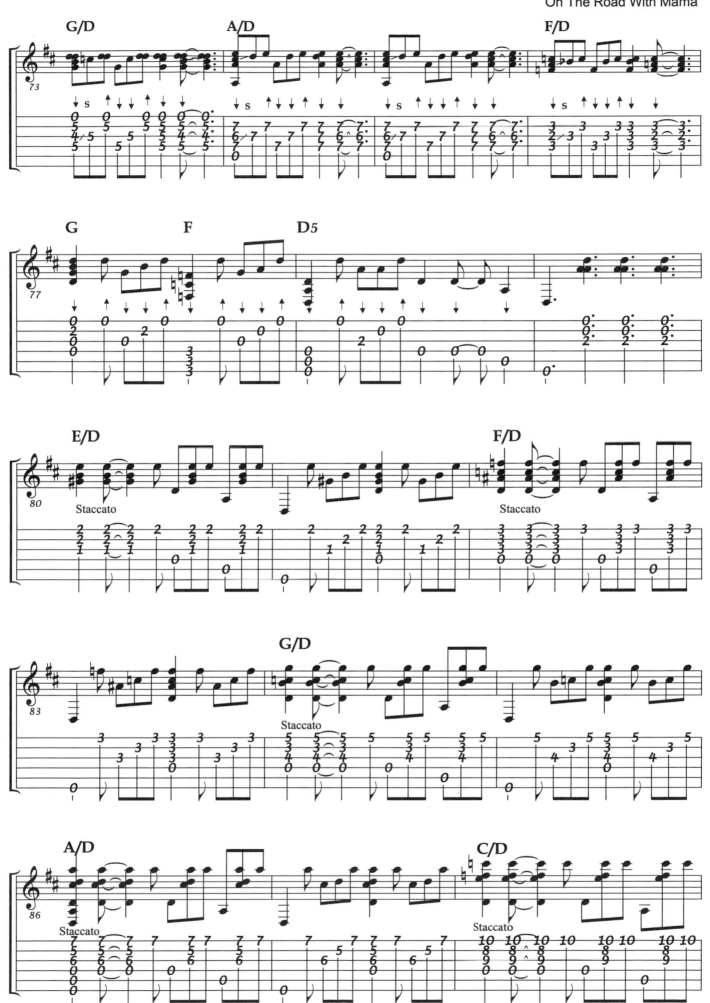

On The Road With Mama

Da 𝄋 alla Coda

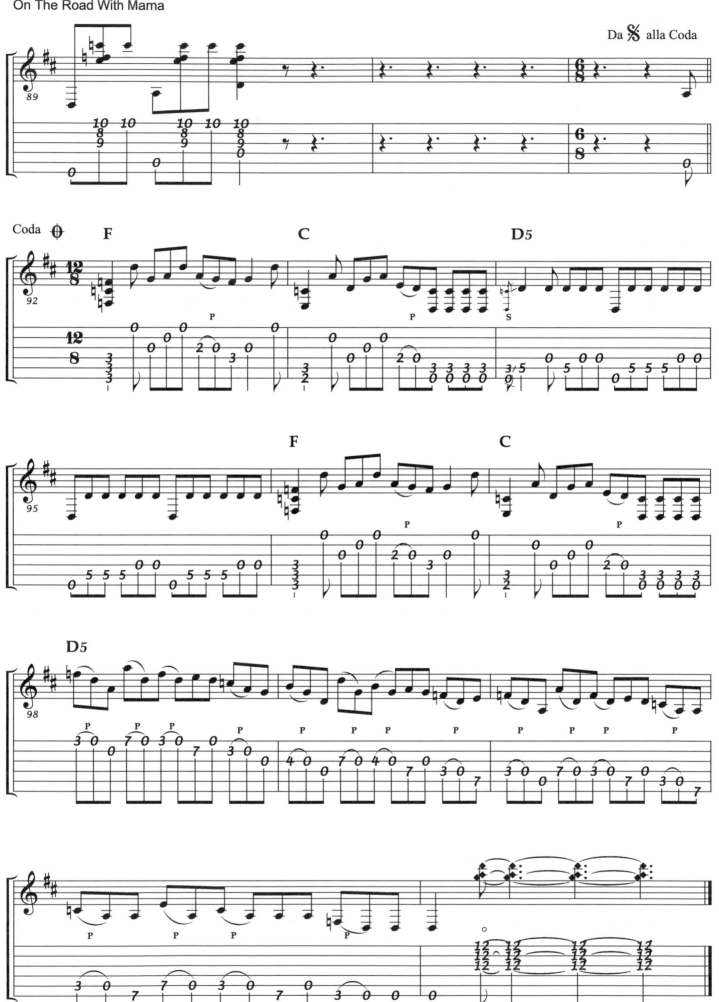

Many of my compositions arise from old folk music models brought back into a modern context.
"Ninna Nonna" is a typical example of this. I am sure that this approach still makes sense, and that it is still possible to express simple and deep thoughts through different kinds of music (the idea behind this tune lies in the concept that it is possible to devote a sweet lullaby even to elderly people).

Ninna Nonna

Tuning: D G D G A D

Capo on the 2nd Fret

Beppe Gambetta

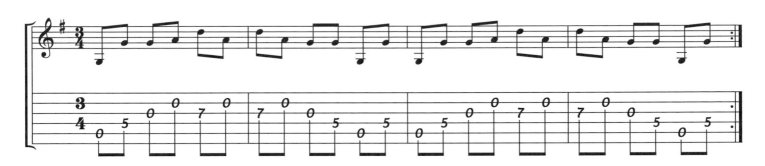

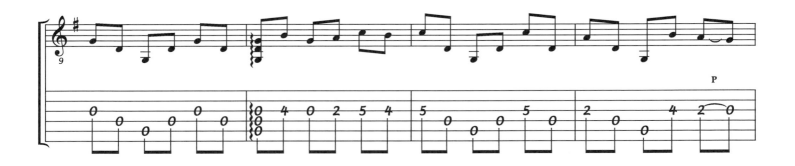

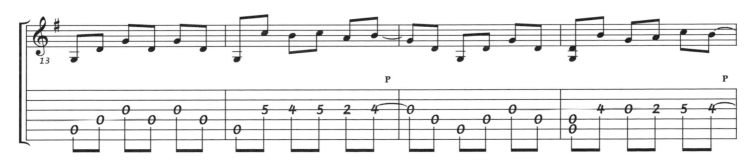

© 2008 Giuseppe Gambetta (SIAE - ITALIA)

Ninna Nonna

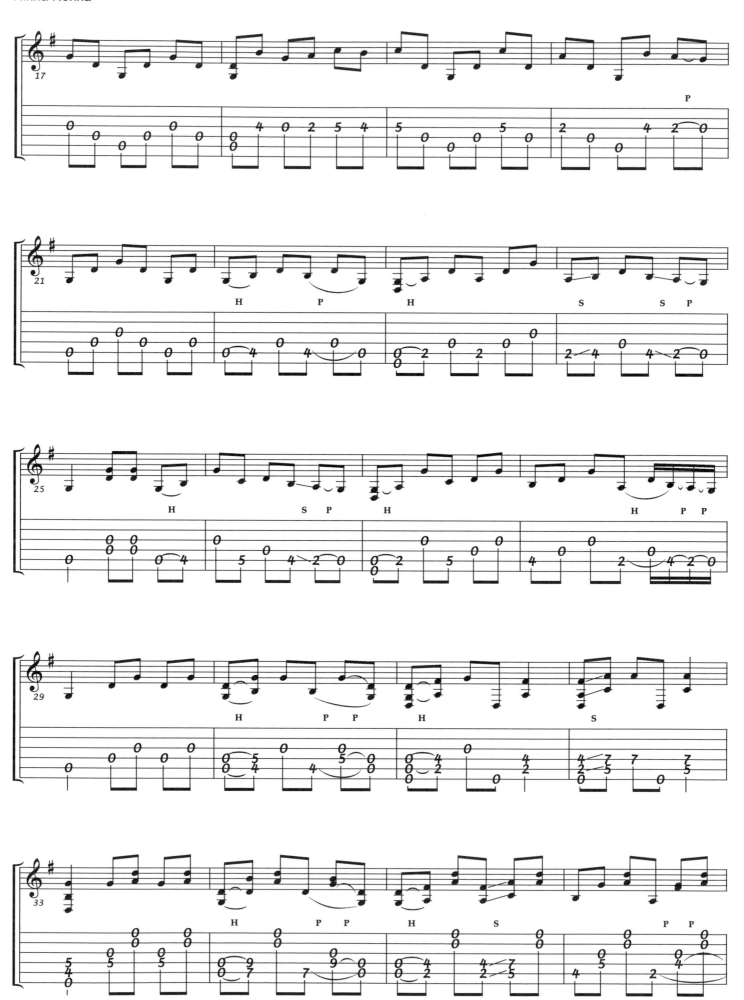

Photo by *Giorgio Scarfi*

Duets

The duet between two acoustic guitars, which creates a beautiful, flawless and complete synergy, is considered the soul of flatpicking. Over the years, this sound has fascinated and thrilled generations of acoustic guitarists even in remote places and cultures alien to the American sound. The origins of this form of music were lost in time and lots of amazing duets were already heard in early country music (e.g. Carter Family, Delmore Brothers, etc.). However, in the history of this style of music, the acoustic duet of excellence is the one between Doc Watson and his son Merle in the memorable studio and live recordings, in which perfect synergy between flatpicking and fingerpicking can be heard.

In my repertoire, the most typical examples of duet can be found in my first LP entitled "Dialogs" (Brambus Records, 1988) recorded on the road in the Eighties with a portable recording device, and in my CD "Synergia" (Thunderation, 2001) with Dan Crary, whose repertoire is specifically aimed at revitalizing the energy of the traditional Brother Duets. The seemingly instinctive spontaneity on which good duets apparently rely hides a great deal of preparation, in which sensitivity to the overall sound plays an important role.

Playing two different melody lines in parallel requires unique concentration, compared to the effort required during a solo or a rhythm back-up, because attention is primarily focused on the timing, which needs to be perfectly synchronized.

The variations that lead to the transition from Carter Style crosspicking create a very interesting effect.

In order to improve your skills, particular attention should be paid (as with any form of ensemble) to being able to listen to the other and to thinking about the overall sound, instead of just focusing on your own performance. The chosen examples are taken from the traditional repertoire. "Blues Ain't Nothin'", in particular, is a good example of how the styles of flatpicking and fingerpicking can melt and integrate to perfection. "Marcia Americana", instead, comes from the repertoire of the great Genoese folk guitarist Pasquale Taraffo (1887-1937) to whom I have dedicated a dutiful revival in my CDs "Serenata" (Acoustic Music Records, 1997) and "Traversata" (Acoustic Disc, 2001).

Recommended Videos and Bibliography:
Pat Donohue, Mike Bowling, *Two Guitars Jamming*,
Homespun Tapes (DVD + TAB)

Recommended Recordings:
Doc & Merle Watson, *Doc Watson On Stage*, Vanguard Records
Norman Blake, Tony Rice, *Blake & Rice*, Rounder 1987
Ricky Skaggs, Tony Rice, *Skaggs & Rice*, Sugar Hill 1980
Beppe Gambetta, *Dialogs*, Brambus Records 1989
Gambetta & Crary, *Synergia*, Thunderation Music 2001
Dan Crary, *Jammed if I do*, Sugar Hill 1994
Bryan Sutton, *Not too far from the tree*, Sugar Hill 2006

Sweet Sunny South

Melody

Traditional,
arranged by Beppe Gambetta

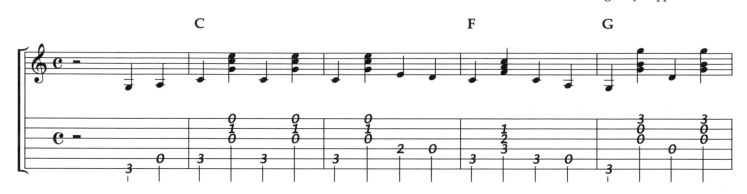

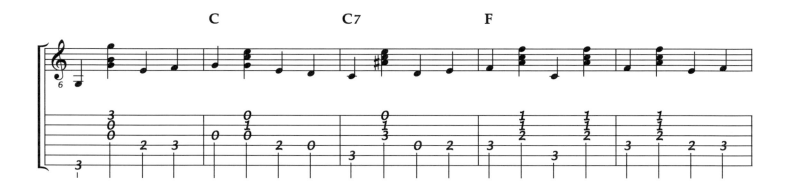

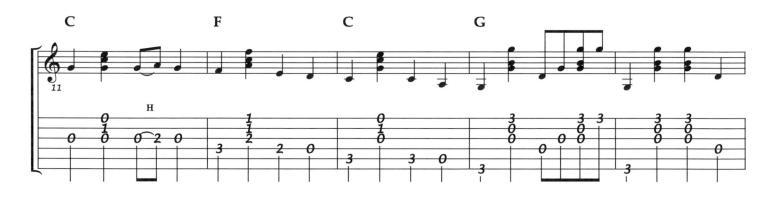

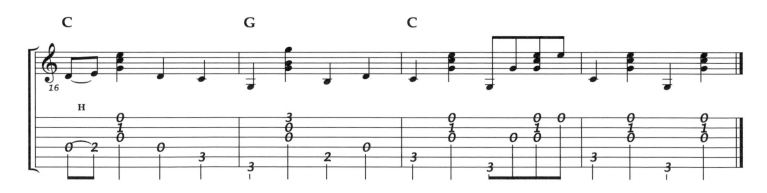

Sweet Sunny South

Harmony

Blues Ain't Nothin'

Fingerpicking

Traditional,
arranged by Beppe Gambetta

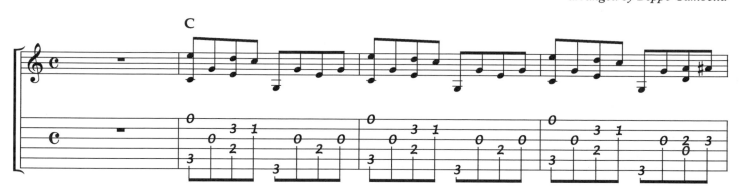

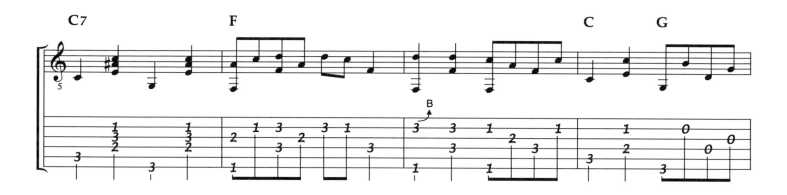

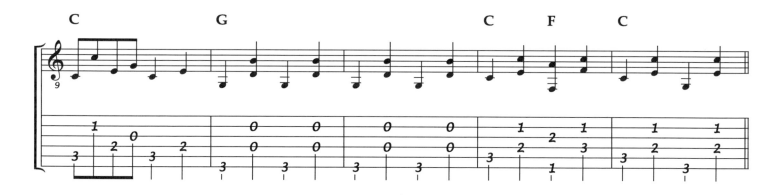

© 2010 Giuseppe Gambetta (SIAE - ITALIA)

Blues Ain't Nothin'

Flatpicking

© 2010 Giuseppe Gambetta (SIAE - ITALIA)

Marcia Americana

Music by Pasquale Taraffo
(Genova 1887 - Buenos Aires 1937)
Arranged by Beppe Gambetta

Beppe's solo

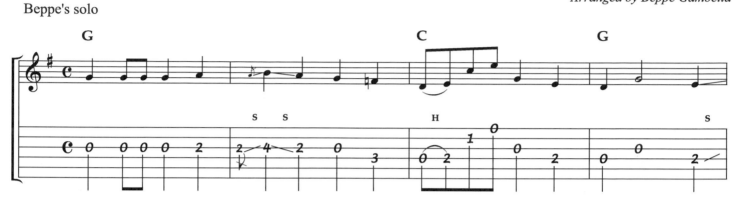

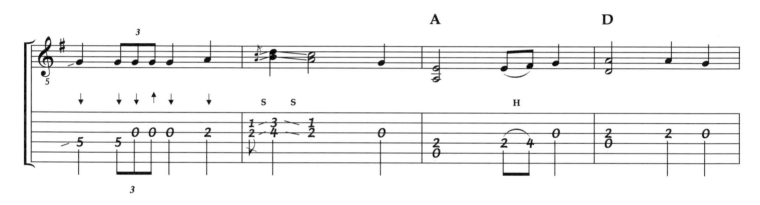

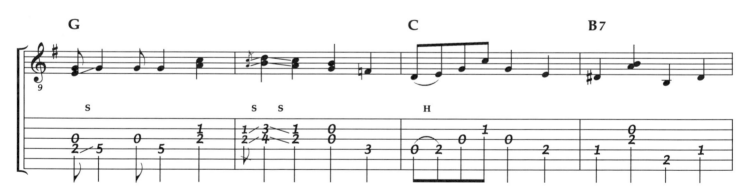

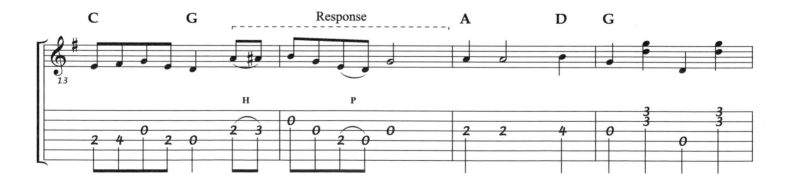

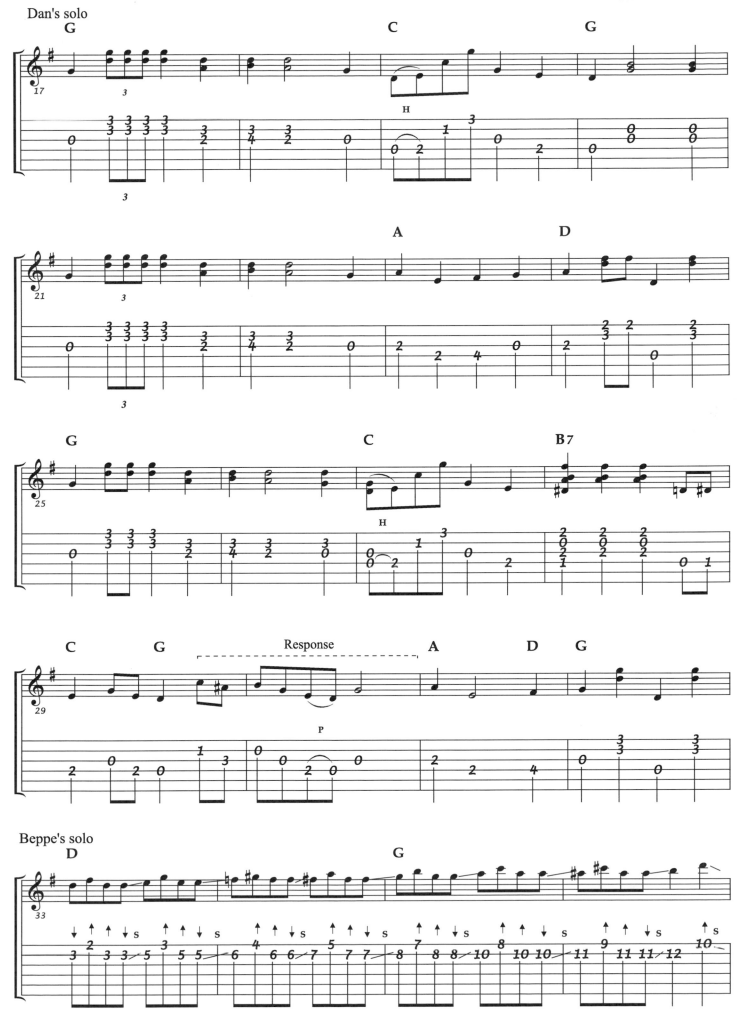

Marcia Americana

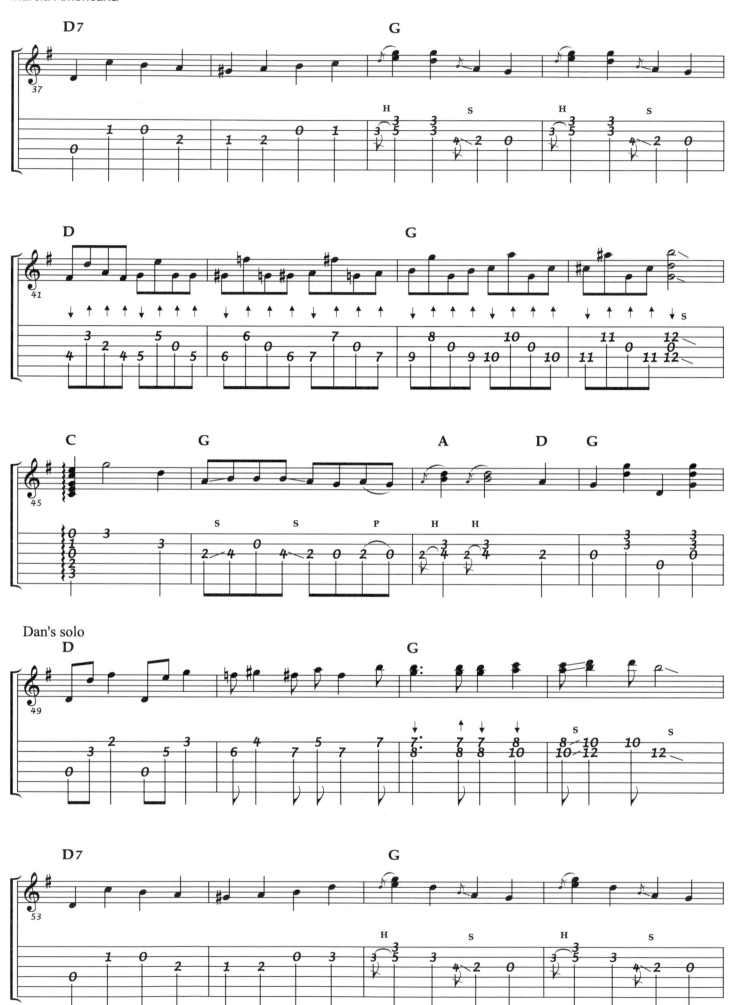

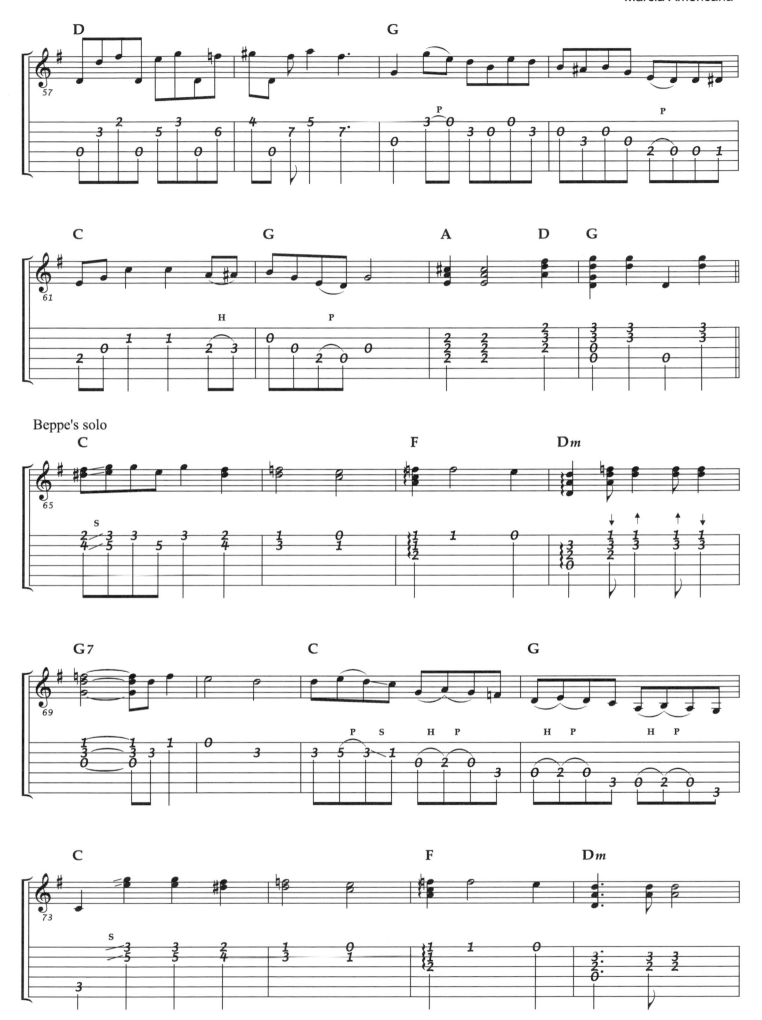

Beppe's solo

Marcia Americana

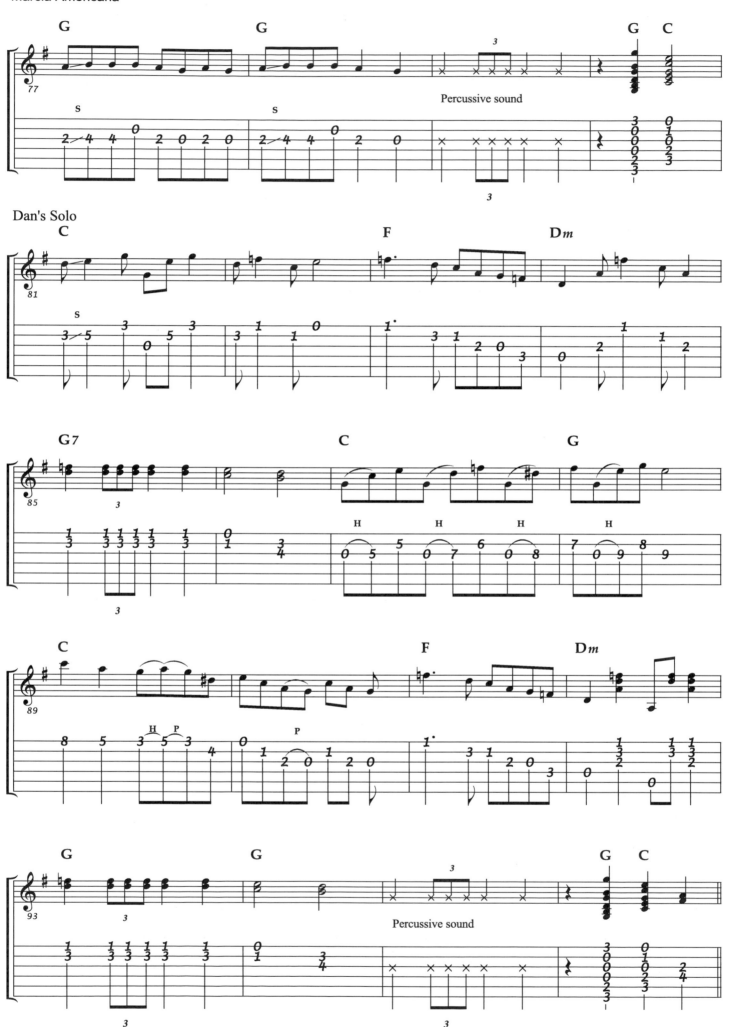

Dan's Solo

168

Beppe's Ending (Melody)

Dan's Ending

Marcia Americana

Under the Double Eagle

Traditional,
arranged by Beppe Gambetta e Dan Crary

Dan's Solo

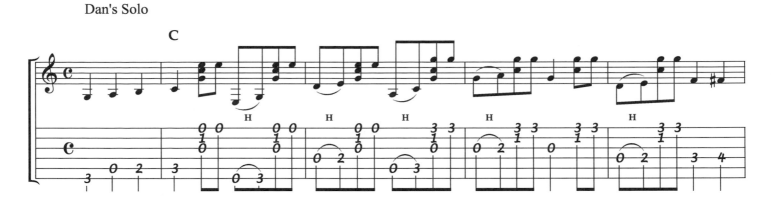

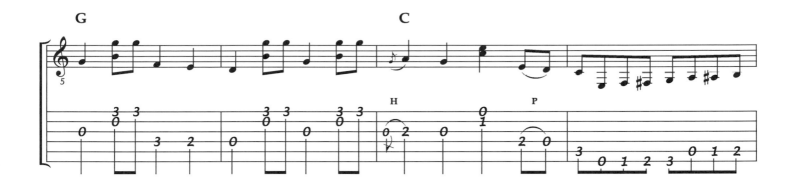

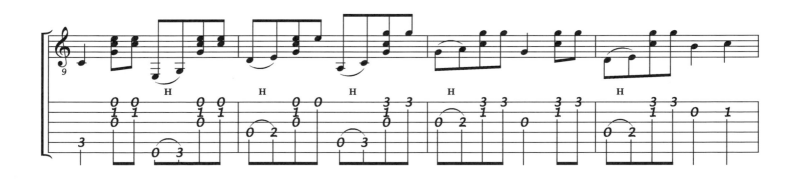

Beppe's Solo

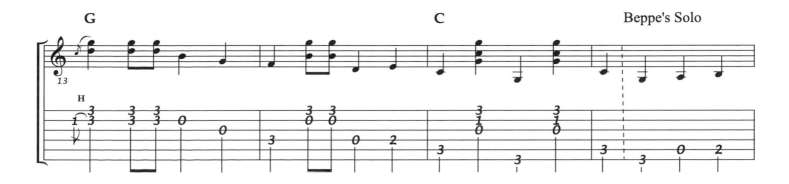

© 2002 Giuseppe Gambetta (SIAE - ITALIA)

Under The Double Eagle

Under The Double Eagle

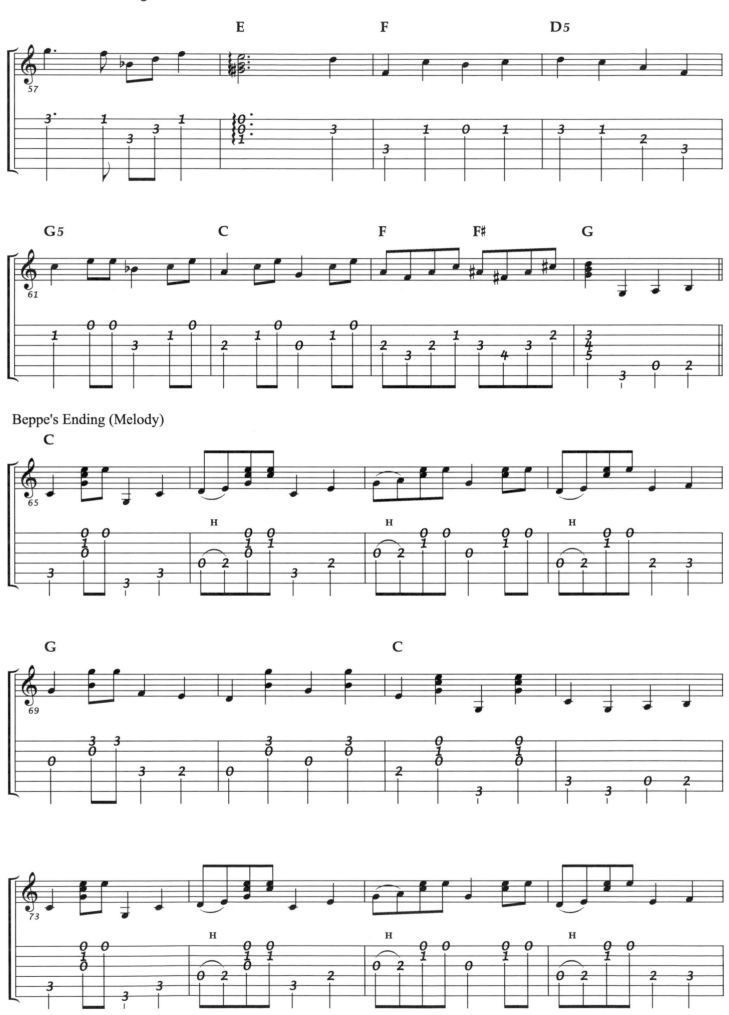

Beppe's Ending (Melody)

Dan's Ending

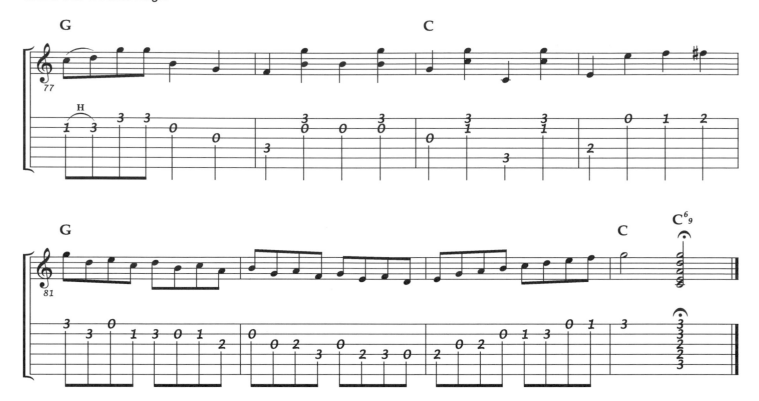

Orchestras

One of the most important contributions of music is bringing people together. Because of its portability and universality, the guitar is one of the best suited tools for this purpose, both at the professional level and, fortunately, even among newest beginners who love this musical instrument.

A group of guitars can play the most diverse musical genres, and has the advantage of allowing, even within the same ensemble, various levels of technical skill. With the right choice of repertoire, guitar orchestras can perform many different kinds of music.

The dynamics between musicians of an orchestra, or group of guitars, is difficult to manage. Often there is an overload of "middle" tones that requires adjustment using arrangement.

It's a good idea to elect or appoint a director. S/he should discuss, take notes, decide on arrangements, conduct rehearsals, set appointments and deadlines.

The following tracks are two of my compositions for ensembles of guitars, which we have already experimented with during my residential seminars. The first is for a beginner-intermediate level. The second presents more difficulties.

> **Recommended Recordings:**
> Los Angeles Guitar Quartet, *Latin*, Telarc, 2002
> Men of Steel, *Four Way Mirror*, Goby Fish Music, 2006

The Petty Thief

First Guitar - Melody

Beppe Gambetta

© 2010 Giuseppe Gambetta (SIAE - ITALIA)

The Petty Thief

Second Guitar

Beppe Gambetta

© 2010 Giuseppe Gambetta (SIAE - ITALIA)

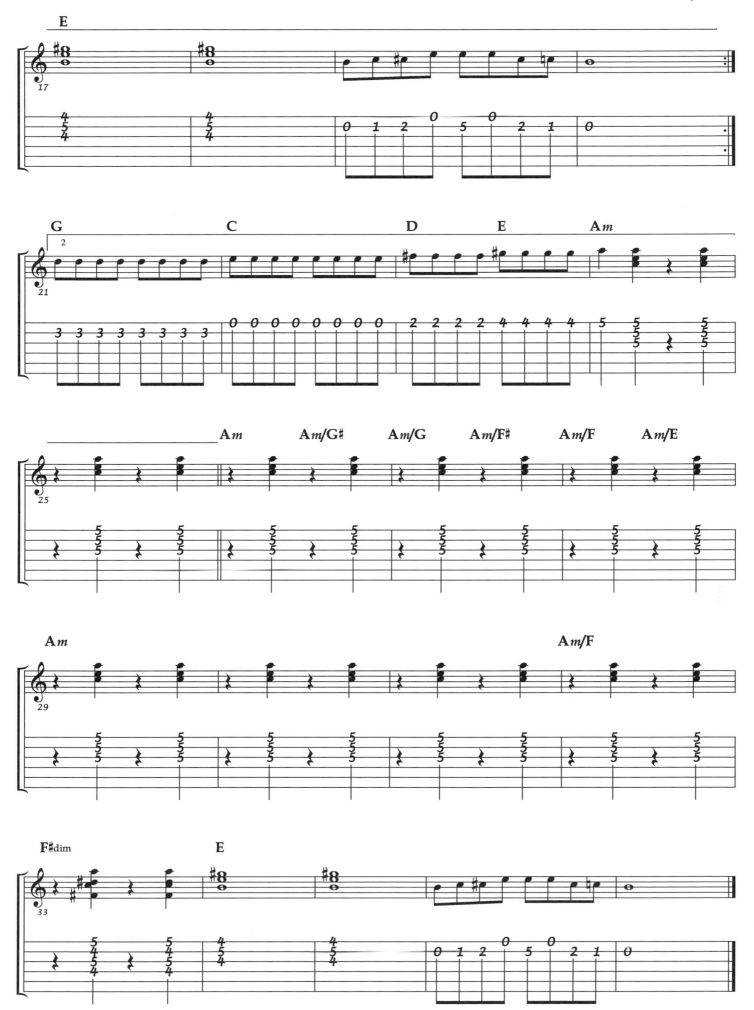

The Petty Thief

Third Guitar

Beppe Gambetta

© 2010 Giuseppe Gambetta (SIAE - ITALIA)

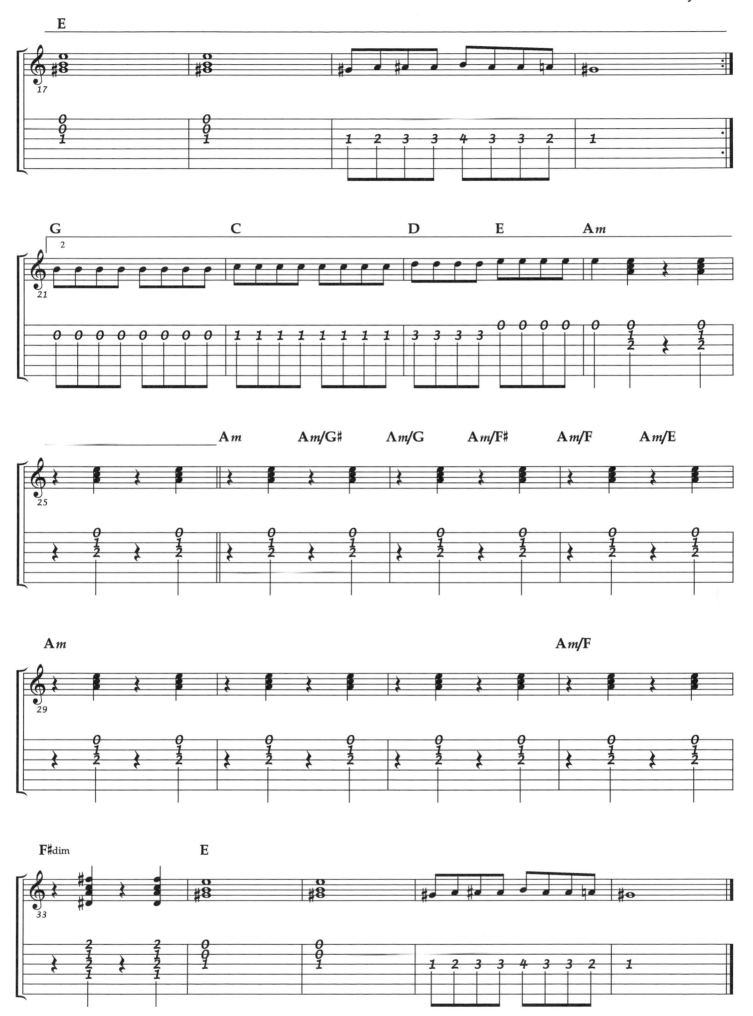

The Petty Thief

Fourth Guitar - Bass Line

Beppe Gambetta

© 2010 Giuseppe Gambetta (SIAE - ITALIA)

Hunterdon Bolero

First guitar - Melody

Beppe Gambetta

© 2006 Giuseppe Gambetta (SIAE - ITALIA)

Hunterdon Bolero

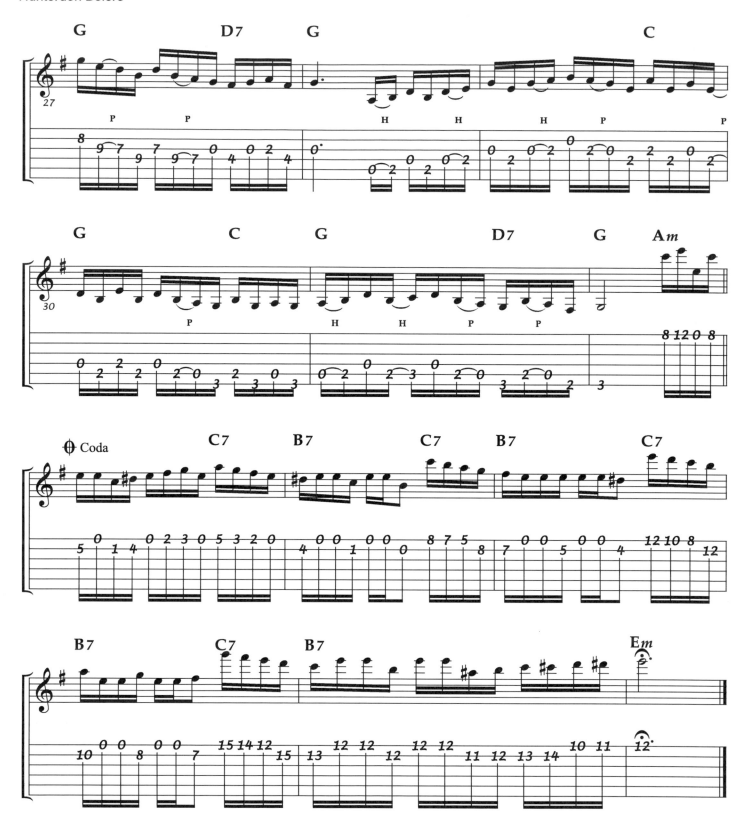

Hunterdon Bolero

Second guitar

Beppe Gambetta

© 2006 Giuseppe Gambetta (SIAE - ITALIA)

Hunterdon Bolero

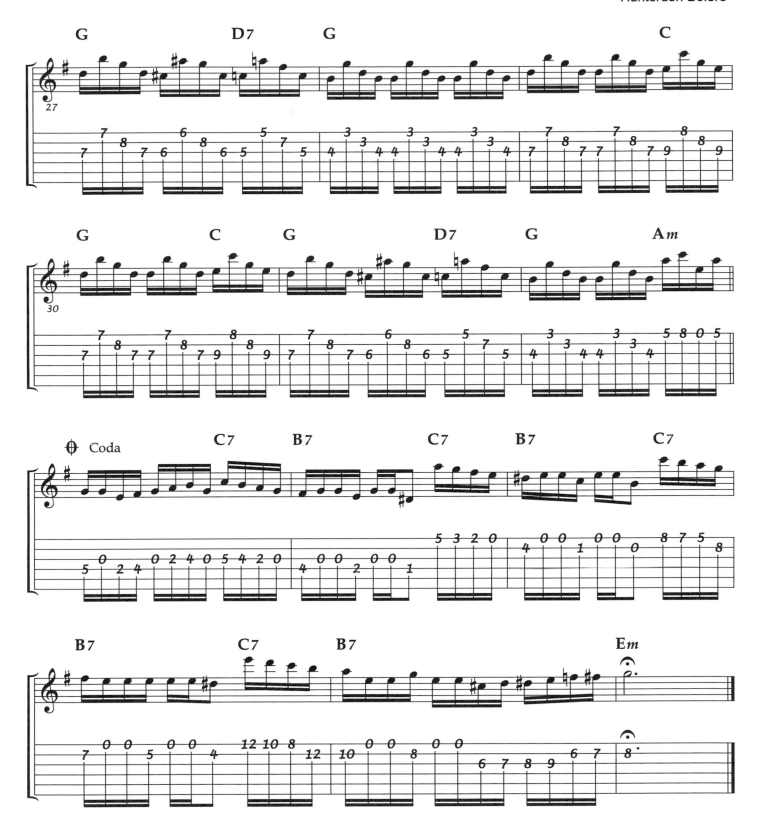

Hunterdon Bolero

Third guitar - Accompaniment

Beppe Gambetta

© 2006 Giuseppe Gambetta (SIAE - ITALIA)

Last time to Coda ⊕

Hunterdon Bolero

Arranging a song means screening it through your own aesthetic sense in order to infuse it with new energy, and give it a new point of view, working with your personal taste to transform it into a new work of art.

Nowadays, if the most beautiful melodies and music seem to have already been composed, a great deal of traditional music is waiting to be re-examined and rediscovered. Sometimes the boring concept of playing cover songs can be overturned by a careful choice of the song to perform: by avoiding the usual clichés, long-forgotten songs can be brought back to life, and thereby revived and passed on to future generations.

Thanks to its portability, the guitar is a unique tool for shaping an arrangement. Despite its limitations, it is an incredibly versatile instrument that can serve both as accompaniment and in a solo role. It is so flexible that it can fit any style. The most common approach is to use a guitar to build the concept of an arrangement, and then put the parts of other instruments alongside. But it is equally challenging to express various atmospheres, variations and shades of sound using just the guitar.

It may appear over-simplistic to draft a non-exhaustive list of essential elements to work on in order to build an arrangement, but it is certainly useful for those who are taking their first steps in this direction.

Initially we're concerned with the fundamental elements: choosing the key, the tempo, the use of an eventual open tuning, rhythm or rhythmic groove changes, electing one or more rhythm patterns. This last element is decisive. Adding a blues, swing or rock feel to the tune involves important changes that need to be carefully considered as they will completely change the flavor of the song.

At that point it is possible to add a new introduction, an ending to the tune, new refrains, new parts and solos, new chords and harmonic variations, a new back-up, melodic elaborations achieved by adding, removing, stretching the tune or changing small details. The personal touch comes, finally, from your performance, the way you feel and play the tune and sing it if it is a song.

The chapter on accompaniment on page 35 already provides a good basis of rhythmic patterns and phrasing to work on. But, in order to provide a comprehensive overview on the topic, I would like to add more elements to the ones described earlier, and comment on some typical examples of arrangement from my repertoire.

The arrangement often gains energy from a good guitar introduction. In every style, and every period in time, we have seen acoustic guitar intros that have made history.

From "Michelle" to "Stairway to Heaven", innumerable songs among the greatest hits have been based on great acoustic intros. When these ideas are strong enough to capture the listener's attention, they are usually called "hooks", in music slang. It is sometimes worthwhile to play those phrases not only at the beginning of the tune, but also at other key points and, perhaps, as the ending. It is interesting to notice that the structure of these intros often have no close relationship with the melody of the song. They usually represent a separate idea that helps add spice to the tune.

Recommended Videos and Bibliography:
Peter Rowan and Tony Rice, *Teach Songs, Guitar and Musicianship*, Homespun Tapes (DVD+TAB)

Recommended Recordings:
Beppe Gambetta, *Blu di Genova*, Gadfly Records, 2002
Alison Krauss, Robert Plant, *Raising Sand*, Rounder, 2007
Darrell Scott, *Theatre of the Unheard*, Full Light Records, 2003
Abigail Washburn, *Abigail Washburn & The Sparrow Quartet*, Nettwerk Records, 2008
Ricky Skaggs & Bruce Hornsby, *Ricky Skaggs & Bruce Hornsby*, Sony Legacy, 2007
Mark Knopfler, *Golden Heart*, WEA/Reprise, 1996

EXAMPLES IN DIFFERENT STYLES

The first example is taken directly from "Hard Travelin'", Woody Guthrie's signature song. I decided to rearrange it, adding a blues feel. The refrain built in DGDGAD tuning works really well along with a slide guitar (as performed in my "Slade Stomp" CD). But it also sounds great on solo guitar. The same refrain used for the intro is repeated at the end of each verse and is also used as the ending of the tune.

Hard Travelin'
Intro

Tuning: D G D G A D

Capo on the 5th fret

Woody Guthrie,
arranged by Beppe Gambetta

New Intro - Refrain

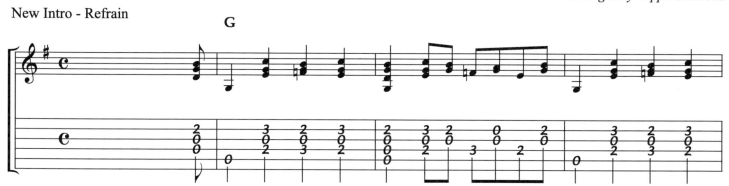

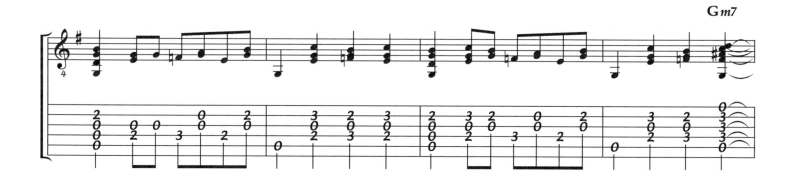

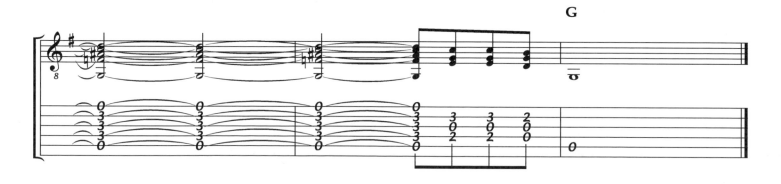

© 2010 Giuseppe Gambetta (SIAE - ITALIA)

The melancholic phrase played in the "Battle of Waterloo" intro is also repeated several times during the song, and is conceived to blend with the lament sung by Patty Larkin.

Battle of Waterloo
Intro

Capo on the 2nd Fret

Traditional,
arranged by Beppe Gambetta

New Intro

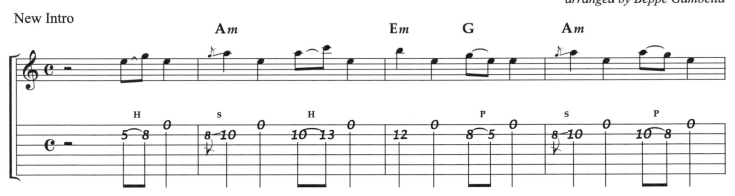

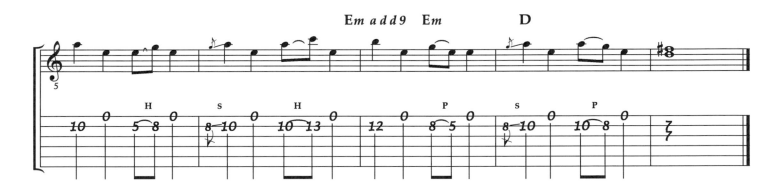

© 2010 Giuseppe Gambetta (SIAE - ITALIA)

An interesting example of rhythm is found in the accompaniment of my version of "Creuza de Ma" (De Andrè/Pagani), where the percussive effect recreates the steps of the sailors who sing while walking to the pub.

Rhythm for
Creuza de Ma

Tuning: D A D G A D

Capo on the 2nd Fret

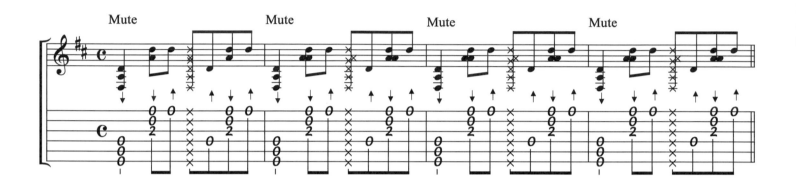

Note: x = Palm percussive effect on all strings

Among the rhythm solutions that I prefer, I suggest using rhythmic lick to accompany the traditional song "Long Journey Home". In the arrangement, a duo, guitarist Dan Crary overlaps my part with regular rhythmic strumming.

Rhythm for
Long Journey Home

Tuning: D A D G A D

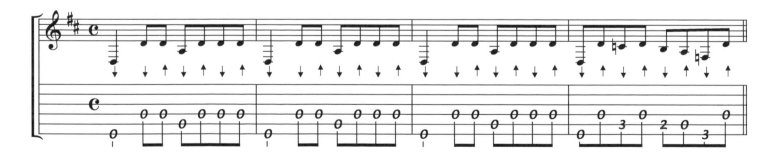

I will now present the entire arrangement of "I'm Worried Now" (from the "Slade Stomp" CD). It is a traditional American song made famous by Doc Watson, with an intro built on an *up-up-down* lick repeated at the end of the two solos. The arrangement is characterized by a key modulation at the beginning and at the end of the second solo, and could end with a medley of traditional songs.

I'm Worried Now

Capo on the 2nd Fret

Traditional,
arranged by Beppe Gambetta

Intro and Refrain

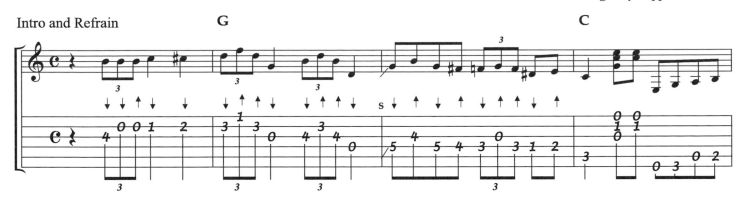

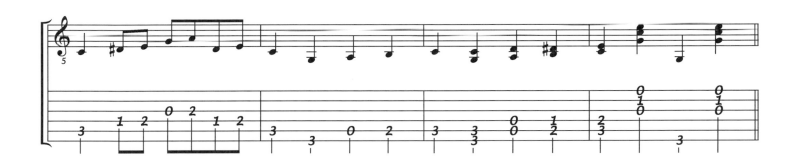

First Solo (in the key of C)

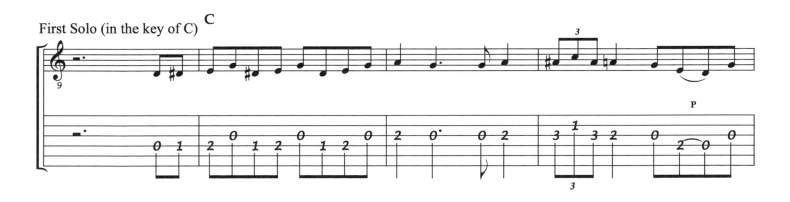

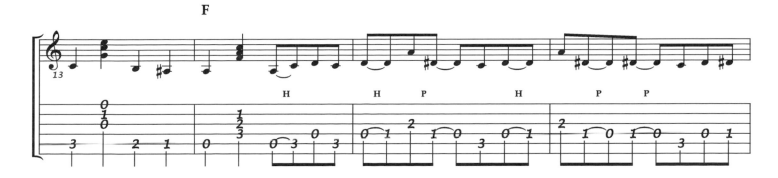

© 2010 Giuseppe Gambetta (SIAE - ITALIA)

I'm Worried Now

Finally, here is the arrangement of "Nova Gelosia/Serenata" (from the "Blu di Genova" CD). "Nova Gelosia" is a composition of the eighteenth century previously put forward by Roberto Murolo and Fabrizio De Andrè. I was lucky enough to interview the last of the old serenade singers, who revealed to me that serenades were often medleys of romantic songs played in different sequences. The idea of arranging a piece of music, combining the old with the new and writing an instrumental serenade in DGDGAD tuning as an interlude to the short verses of "Nova Gelosia" comes from those conversations.

Nova Gelosia

Tuning: D G D G A D

Capo on the 3rd fret

Anonymous,
arranged by Beppe Gambetta

Chords in D G D G A D tuning

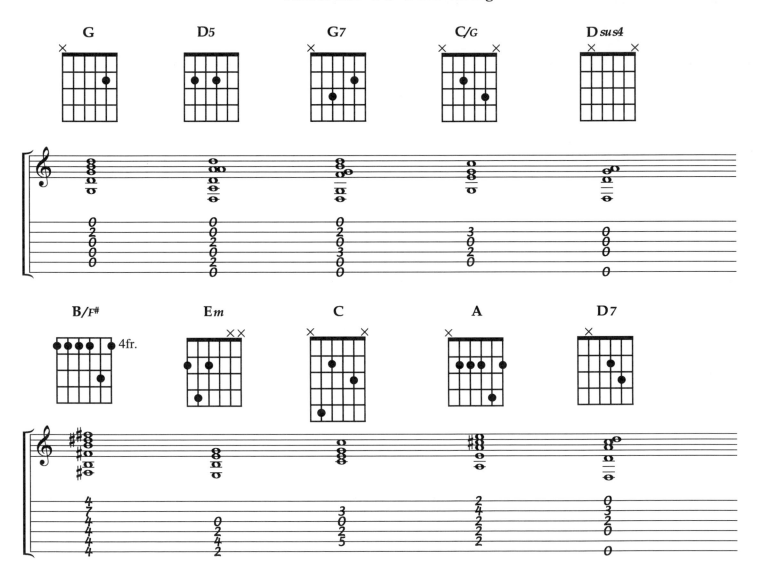

Chord Progression

First Verse

G / D5 / G / G / G7 / C/G / Dsus4 / D5 / G / B/F Em / C / G / A D7 / G / G /

Second Verse

D5 / D5 / G / G / D5 / D5 / G / G / G / B/F Em / C / G / A D7 / G / G /

© 2010 Giuseppe Gambetta (SIAE - ITALIA)

Serenata

Tuning: D G D G A D

Capo on the 3rd fret

Music by Beppe Gambetta

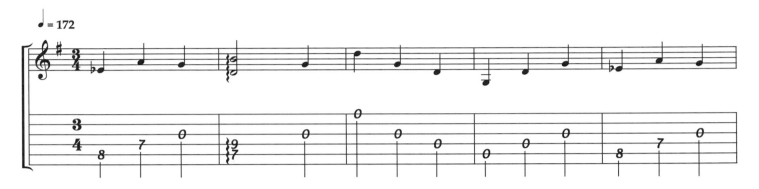

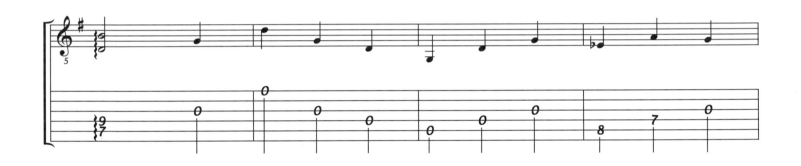

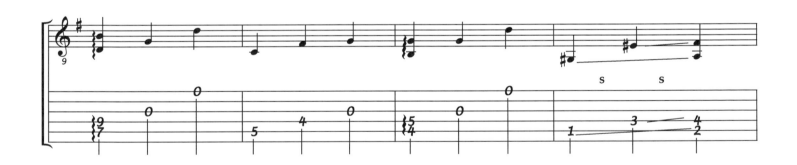

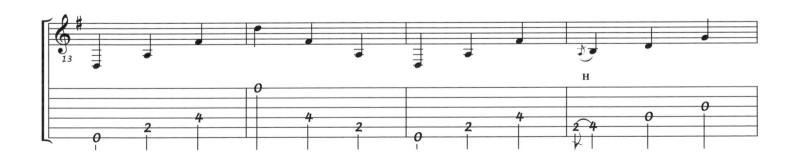

© 2010 Giuseppe Gambetta (SIAE - ITALIA)

Serenata

Serenata

RHYTHMIC GROOVES

I would like to conclude with a long sequence of rhythmic fragments that represent the foundation of many arrangements. It is an invitation to work, create and compose that also refers to the previous chapter, as these grooves are a good starting point for an ensemble of only guitars.

I have now come to the end of this work, and, hopefully, I have left out very little. I hope this method will help you to love and enjoy music as I do, and I wish you a life filled with art and poetry.

Latin *Groove*

Beppe Gambetta

© 2010 Giuseppe Gambetta (SIAE - ITALIA)

Blues *Groove*

Beppe Gambetta

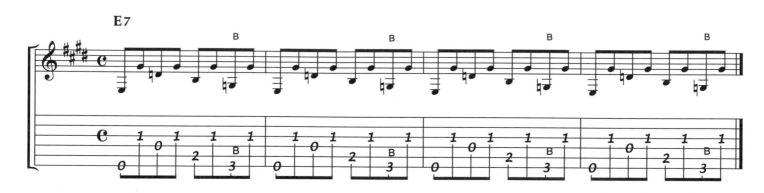

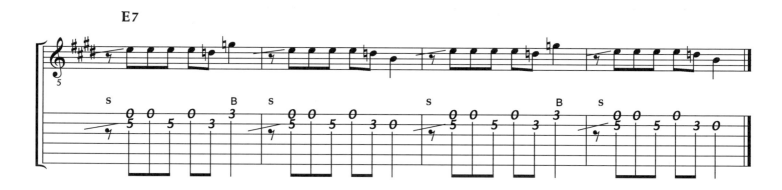

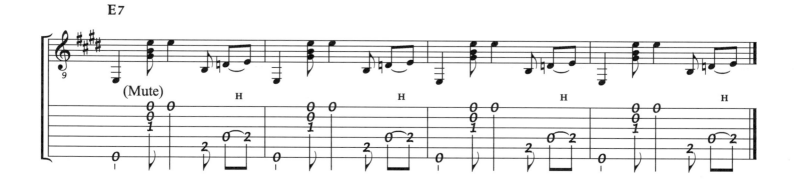

© 2010 Giuseppe Gambetta (SIAE - ITALIA)

Balkan *Groove*

Beppe Gambetta

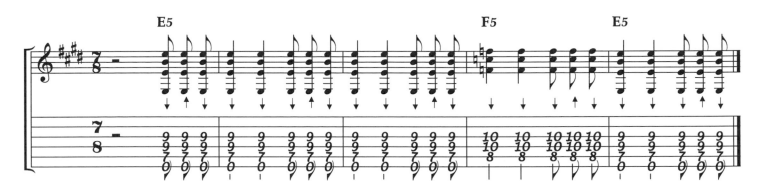

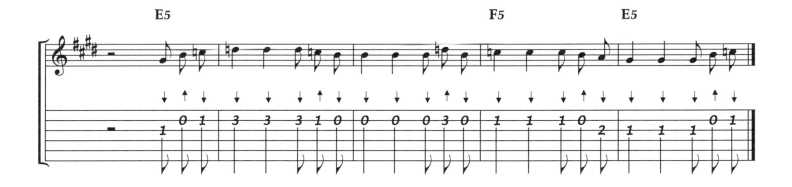

© 2010 Giuseppe Gambetta (SIAE - ITALIA)

Western Swing Groove

Beppe Gambetta

© 2010 Giuseppe Gambetta (SIAE - ITALIA)

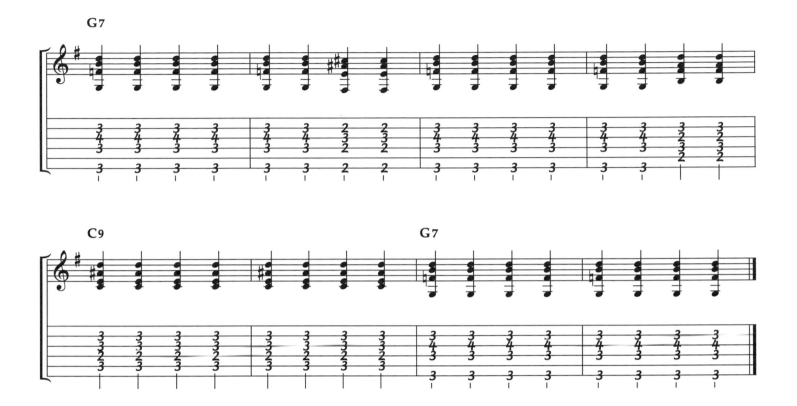

Cajun *Groove*

Beppe Gambetta

© 2010 Giuseppe Gambetta (SIAE - ITALIA)

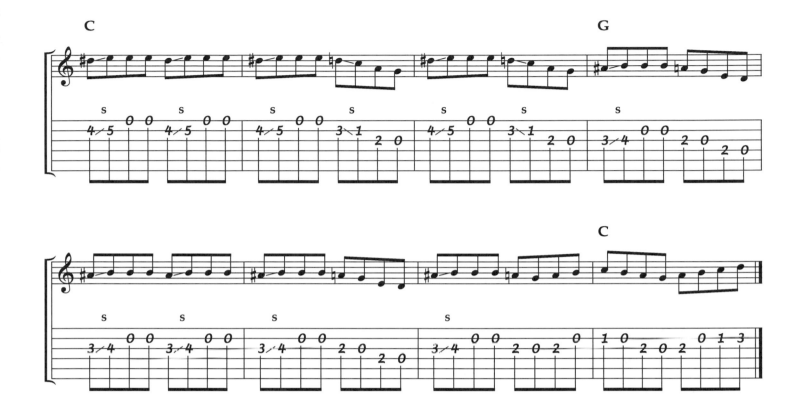

Spanish *Groove*

Beppe Gambetta

© 2010 Giuseppe Gambetta (SIAE - ITALIA)

Hawaiian *Groove*

Beppe Gambetta

© 2010 Giuseppe Gambetta (SIAE - ITALIA)